AND STILL FLYING...

LIFE AND TIMES
Elizabeth "Betty" Wall
W.A.S.P.   W.W. II

by Patrick Roberts

"Elizabeth Strohfus is an incredible person. She has had opportunities to do and see things that many of us only dream about. It is amazing to look at the accomplishments she has achieved over a lifetime and it is an honor to know her. Elizabeth is a star that continues to burn bright and is full of more energy than most teenagers. Who else can say they have flown an F-16 at age 71 and a B-17 at age 82?"

Jon Velishek
Historian
Rice County Historical Society
Faribault, Minnesota

Tony Evans

Second Edition

Walking Shadow Publications
PO Box 444
Faribault MN
55021
USA

Order this book online at www.trafford.com
or email orders@trafford.com

Most Trafford titles are also available at major online book retailers.

Print information available on the last page.

ISBN: 978-1-4120-1313-0 (sc)

Trafford rev. 08/16/2023

North America & international
toll-free: 844-688-6899 (USA & Canada)
fax: 812 355 4082

Dedication

For my real heroes
the combat veterans
and for all they have given.

Prologue

By-Laws
Of
Women Airforce Service Pilots, WW II

Article II

Purpose

The purposes for which this corporation was organized are:
The association of all living women pilots who trained, flew,
and served as pilots with the United States Army Air Forces
during World War II.

To meet regularly in convention to honor the memory of our
comrades who lost their lives in service, to renew old friendships,
and to participate in activities which the Corporation believes will
be of benefit to the nation or the community in which they meet
and to the members of the corporation.

The Corporation shall have power to do all legal acts in furtherance
of its charitable, educational, literary, benevolent, social and historical
purposes, and to administer funds for such purposes.

Foreword

As this project came to life, and as I traveled with Liz to many sites – some quite exotic - I became interested in what determined or shaped the character and dedication of that great generation. Focusing on the WASP's I have made a modest attempt at bringing the realities of the times, the international situations, the black and white world of the first half of the Century and the many innovations and inventions into play that may have had some bearing on the evolving nature of the national consciousness during those decades.

Relating a time-line directly to the years of growth, development and involvement in an uncertain world, I had hoped some connection between the surround and the action might become evident. Words like discipline, respect, moral standards and high-minded echoed throughout the process.

Also, I gave a listing of Elizabeth's presentations, meetings and other outings to give the reader some idea of the energy, dedication and enthusiasm of this octogenarian.

Patrick Roberts

Photography/Graphic Design
Tony Evans, Photographer
(612) 759-1733

Photo credits:

Tony Evans
U.S. National Archives
Senate Historical Department
Owatonna Degner Regional Airport
TP: Images of American Political History
NASA & the Space Telescope Science Institute
Bethlehem Academy Catholic High School Archives

Table of Contents

PART I The Early Years

PART II Life Begins at 70

PART I
THE EARLY YEARS

**1903
First Flight
The Wright
Brothers**

DATE LINE

1903 First showing of "The Wizard of Oz" as a musical
     at New York's Majestic Theater

1905 Aspirin is introduced in America from Britain after
     being discovered in Germany

1906 The Juke Box and Cornflakes appear and cocaine
     is replaced by caffeine in Coca-Cola

1910 Bessica Raiche made solo flight using an aircraft
     she and her husband Francois built

1911 Harriet Quimby became the first woman to be licensed
     as an aeronaut

1912 Henry Ford starts assembly line to build the Model T Ford

1915 Albert Einstein publishes the General Theory of Relativity

WW I battle

W.W. I 1914-1918

1918 German physicist, Max Plank, announced his
     Quantum Theory of Physics, suggesting that sub-atomic
     particles absorb and release energy in units called quanta

1918 The 11th hour, 11th day, 11th month. Armistice signed
     between Allied Powers and Germany

1919 Ernest Rutherford demonstrated the possibility
     of splitting the atom

1919 Elizabeth Bridget Wall was born

1920 First election allowing women the right to vote

1920 The hand-held hair dryer was introduced

1920 The League of Nations came into being

1921 London to Paris air travel began

1921 Insulin was discovered

**Suffragette
Parade
NYC 1918**

**3 Women Voters
1920**

Albert Einstein

**"Modern"
Transportation
The Wall Family**

GROWING TO FLY

The year was 1919 and the country was still rebounding from WW I. As the men went off to fight the 'war to end all wars' the women went off to the factories and other support positions to aid in the war effort. It was estimated that over 30 million men were either killed or wounded during WW I. An entire generation of young men was lost, gone forever. As the men returned from war and back to their jobs, the women, not wanting to be displaced from their new found occupations, became disgruntled (Yes even then!) and began a stronger movement for women's right to vote.

One of the all-time monumental amendments to the Constitution was ratified on January 16, 1919: the Volstad Act – prohibition. Bootlegging, gambling and gang warfare become the theme of "The Roaring Twenties" and women did win their right to vote by passage of the 19th amendment on August 18th, 1920.

It was on November 15th, 1919 that Elizabeth Bridget Wall was born. The 20's was the decade that Elizabeth received her earliest training and education as she started Immaculate Conception Grade School, unaware of and untouched by this other world. Women's worth and involvement in all areas became more in evidence with each passing year. With this setting of the stage, here is the story of Elizabeth Bridget "Betty Wall" Strohfus.

I was really looking forward to my first days at school because, with three older sisters and a brother already students, I learned early on that there was a new world beginning with this school business. I had to dress nicely, meet with the neighborhood 'gang' early in the morning and walk off to school. They would talk "smart", learn new things that they thought made them important, and met many new friends. Sometimes my brother and sisters would bring their new mates home with them and other times they would go to their homes for dinner and spend the night. I could sense that this was going to be a good adventure. While attending Immaculate Conception grade school, I had very few changes of new clothing, but having three older sisters, I was always in line for hand-me-downs.

The nuns ran a well-disciplined 'ship' and we marched together to church and out to the playground. We were taught to respect our elders and to practice the 'Golden Rule'. We were told over and over again that whether a job was big or small, to do it well or not at all, and if you didn't have something nice to say about someone, then don't say anything at all. The school furnished our books and although there was tuition, large families received assistance. Father Foley, our pastor, was very good to us knowing that our father was older and couldn't do much work any more.

Women workers in ordnance shop, 1918

Daniel, Julia and Elizabeth Bridget Wall, 1919

Mother M. Gertrude

3

Father Foley

Uncles Tom & Johnny

Cousins

Mother and father had married late in life; my father was 59 when I came along, making our cousins more like aunts and uncles. I remember our Uncle John Lorem who lived with and took care of our Aunt Maggie. She had polio as a child and was severely crippled, or physically challenged. He worked at the flour mill in town and had tried to start a labor union. In those days, trying to form a union was one of the least popular and most hazardous activities you could imagine. Owners and management alike frowned at the very thought of unions and believed them to be part of a communist plot and a menace to our society. Not to mention their own positions and pocketbooks. Johnny was labeled as a troublemaker, fired, and 'blackballed' from employment anywhere in the area. He had to make a living somehow for himself and Aunt Maggie, so he mastered the art of 'fermenting the grape' so to speak, and practiced the 'speak-easy' business of bootlegging.

At the time, the superintendent of schools lived next door to Johnny and he had complained to the Sheriff that something 'fishy' was going at Lorem's house because of the great number of visitors both day and night. The Sheriff, not only being a good friend of John's but also a regular customer, warned John that he was coming to raid his home the next day. Uncle John had a big pantry with a basement underneath it. He had a rug over the trap door and a table on top of the rug. His 'still' was taken apart and, with all his other brewing paraphernalia, was spirited away to the basement. Sure enough, the next day the Sheriff showed up with his deputy and the superintendent. They searched the house high and low and they came up dry –literally! The Sheriff looked that superintendent right straight in the eye and said with great sincerity, "Johnny must have a great number of very good friends."
And that was that.

When Johnny got his 'still' up and bubbling again, he used to 'invite' us kids to come over and suck on a tube to siphon the hooch into big old jugs. All the sludge settled at the bottom of the vat and was the first stuff to come out. That 'gunk' was fouler tasting than I could ever express. I escaped this chore by telling Uncle John that I had taken the 'pledge', a solemn oath, and could never touch the liquor again or that I'd go straight
to hell for sure. And that was that.

Liz taking the "Pledge"

To supplement this income, he also sold fish to the Catholics on Fridays. As the story goes (and I should say again, story), he always had a pushcart full of fresh fish on Friday outside the church. Too many fish for any one person to possibly have caught. The school superintendent, still certain there was something 'fishy' going on over at Lorem's house, pointed this overabundance of fish out to the game warden, hoping to catch him at this game. The warden, also a regular customer of Johnny's other enterprise, promised to check it out. One Thursday

Grade School Graduation

he staked out the dock at Kelly-Dudley Lake where John launched his little duck-skiff. With the warden observing from the blind, sure enough, John rowed out to the middle of the lake, lit a half stick of dynamite from his cigar and tossed it over the side. He netted a great number of sunfish, bluegills, bullheads and a few walleye. As John approached the dock, the warden stepped out from behind the trees and explained why he was there while helping secure the boat to the dock. With one foot on the dock and the other in the skiff, Johnny slowly back paddled until the warden had to jump into the boat before landing in the drink. The warden kept citing the law while trying to figure out an angle to help get Johnny out of this mess while Johnny kept on paddling. In the middle of the lake, John calmly lit another stick of dynamite, handed it to the warden and said, "fish or shut-up!" And that was that.

While our father was still alive, his two brothers stayed with us in their old age and mother took care of them until they died. Those were different times and showed the true spirit of a loving extended family. If at all possible, no relative was ever put out to 'pasture' or into the poor house. Uncle Tom arrived in 1922 and lived with us until his death. Uncle John then moved in and he stayed another few years. Our brother George had to give up his room for the elders and slept on the couch

President Lincoln

in the parlor while the five of us girls had one room up stairs set up like a dormitory. Just how long ago those times actually were is evidenced by the fact that my father was three years old when President Lincoln gave the Gettysburg Address and President Ulysses S. Grant had signed the Land Grant for my grandfather's property near Veseli, MN.

U.S. Grant

The United States of America,

To all to whom these presents shall come, Greeting:

Homestead Certificate No. _75_

Application _127_

Whereas, there has been deposited in the **General Land Office** of the United States, a CERTIFICATE of the Register of the Land Office at _St. Peter_ , whereby it appears that pursuant to the Act of Congress approved 20th May, 1862, "To secure Homesteads to actual Settlers on the public domain," and the acts supplemental thereto, the claim of _Daniel Wall_ has been established and duly consummated in conformity to law for the _North East quarter of Section twelve, in Township One Hundred and Twelve North of Range Twentytwo West, in the District of lands subject to sale at St. Peter Minnesota containing One Hundred and Sixty acres_

according to the Official Plat of the Survey of the said Land returned to the **General Land Office** by the Surveyor General.

Now know ye, That there is therefore granted by the UNITED STATES unto the said _Daniel Wall_ the tract of Land above described: **To Have and to Hold** the said tract of Land, with the appurtenances thereof, unto the said _Daniel Wall_ and to _his_ heirs and assigns forever.

In testimony whereof, I, _Ulysses S. Grant_ , PRESIDENT OF THE UNITED STATES OF AMERICA, have caused these letters to be made Patent, and the Seal of the General Land Office to be hereunto affixed.

Given under my hand, at the CITY OF WASHINGTON, the _first_ day of _September_ , in the year of our Lord one thousand eight hundred and _Sixtynine_ , and of the INDEPENDENCE OF THE UNITED STATES the _Ninetyfourth_

By the President: _U. S. Grant_

By _J. M. Merritt_ , Secy

J. Granger , Recorder of the General Land Office

**Land Grant dated September 1, 1869
Signed by President U.S. Grant**

THE WALL FAMILY 1922

Daniel and Julia Anne in back of Elizabeth Bridget, George, Mary, Catherine and Julia circling Cecelia on the throne.

I was number five in a family of 6 children and I'd like to introduce the others. Mary, the eldest, was born in 1913 followed by our one brother George who arrived in 1915. Catherine came to be in 1916 and Julie came along in 1918. Then there was me in 1919, and the last shall come first with Cecelia in 1922. Quite a statement considering my father was 61 and mother 40 when Cece was born. In looking back, we had a normal, happy life. We never knew we were poor and seldom had a dull moment. I am not sure if the stock market crash affected us or not, but the closing of the banks sure did. Father had sold his farms before marrying mother and thankfully he had paid for our house. We had a home but not much more.

I kept hearing that we were poor but I never realized just how poor we were until I grew up. Having been a farmer all his life, father had a glorious vegetable garden and a chicken coop in our back yard and we would sit in his garden with a salt shaker and enjoy the tomatoes. We had a root cellar in the basement where we packed the potatoes, beets and onions in dirt filled bins in one corner. I remember a big crock of sauerkraut 'brewing' all the time. What a terrible smell but what a wonderful taste. I guess having a roof over our heads, clothes to wear and food to eat we lived quite well. Of course mother baked fresh bread and especially good doughnuts weekly.

Picnic with the nuns

Mary

Catherine

Julia, George & Catherine

Hoboes would come to the back door of our home for handouts and there was always something for them. We became quite a popular stop on their tour. Life was good; we always had enough to eat and a place to lay our heads. Maybe that is why I never realized how poor we were. We seldom had discipline problems other than the necessary reprimands for mischief at which children excel. None of us ever gave a thought to disobey or to talk back to our parents. That just was not part of the equation and, though he never used it, daddy left his shaving strap, a most impressive strap of leather, hanging on the sink in the kitchen. I was never sure whether he left it there for his convenience or to serve as a constant reminder to us for what could happen.

We did have a wonderful childhood and always kept ourselves busy. In those days, we hemmed, mended, darned, cooked, baked, cleaned and studied. But we always found time to play, and could we play. In my younger years, Irene Morgan – now Bosshart - was my best friend, along with my sisters of course, and we played all the popular games of that time. There was hide and seek, kick the can and jump rope. Another game was 'anti-anti-high-over' where you threw a ball over a house to someone on the other side and 'statue' where you whirled the 'it' person around a couple of times and when someone yelled stop, the 'it' person had to hold that position. We sometimes saw 7some rather strange positions but we always had some 'belly-busting"laughs.

Then there was baseball. I was a 'pretty good' pitcher, if I say so myself, and once the west end girls beat the west end boys in a really big game. At other times Irene, Marion Steele, Dorothy Bailey, my sisters Cecelia and Julie and me would act out plays or our 'shows' as we liked to call them. I remember seeing Peggy Shannon perform in "Number Please." Oh, that was exciting. We found a cardboard box, punched holes in it and then put numbers in it and took turns being Peggy. We played by the hours. We used our imaginations and did we have active imaginations!

In the winter we would use pieces of tin to slide down any hill we could find. I would slide down Lucius Smith's terraced lawn and come home drenched. (My sister Mary and I worked for Lucius in his law office years later). I also liked to mound a big pile of snow, dig a hole in it and pretend it was my home. I loved the great out doors and, regardless of the weather, spent many, many hours out in it. I guess I was a tomboy because I mostly liked the things boys did. I wasn't much for dolls and play make-up, dress-up. I loved to climb and get high; I could never get up high enough - and you know the kind of high I'm talking about.

I recall being called into the house for dinner by Mother. She would look around the yard and yell, "all right George, Mary, Kay, Julie and Cecelia, come in for dinner now." And then she would start looking up, up in the trees, up on the neighbor's barn roof or up on our own roof and ask, "and where in the world are you, Elizabeth?"

Our neighborhood gang loved to tell ghost stories. We would walk to the library, look up the scariest stories we could find and take turns telling them. It was so wholesome and such great fun living in those years. Life was slow and not at all complicated.

It was scary for me to go off to the public high school after eight years of well-disciplined schooling at Immaculate Conception. At High School the students did not have to be quiet in between classes and I heard too many wisecracks about some of the teachers. What ever happened to respecting your elders? I was amazed at the noise and could not understand the attitude of so many of the students. I became very shy and didn't mingle with anyone unless I knew them. I was an average student and always tried to stay in the background.

DATE LINE

1925 Louis Armstrong turns jazz into an art form
1925 Hitler writes "Mein Kampf" (my struggle)
     a strategy for world domination
1926 The first liquid fueled rocket is launched by Robert Goddard
1927 Introduced the first Laurel and Hardy film
1927 The first trans-Atlantic flight by Charles Lindberg
     from New York to Paris took 33 hours at an average
     speed of 107.5 mph.
1927 Gangsters who took control of liquor, gambling,
     prostitution and lottery rackets, estimated that
     Al Capone made $105 million in 1927 alone
1928 Penicillin was introduced by Scottish Chemist
     Alexander Flemming
1928 Stalin gains control of Russia
1929 New York Stock Exchange Crash
1929 First Academy Awards awarded in Hollywood on May 16

1929 Charles and Anne Lindberg conduct aerial archeological study over S.E. United States and the Mayan ruins in Central America

Liz & Julia

Cecelia

Al Capone

THE ROARING TWENTIES
CAME TO A SUDDEN HALT WITH THE
OCTOBER 24, 1929
NEW YORK STOCK EXCHANGE CRASH

Coal mining lads

Banks and businesses failed. Millions lost all their savings. American economy in an all-encompassing recession and soon other countries followed the U.S. into the SLUMP.

1930 British aviatrix, Amy Johnson, flew solo from Britain
    to Australia. 10,000 miles in 19 days making Johnson
    a role model for women around the world

1931 Empire State Building opens. Worlds' Tallest building
    at 1,245 feet

1932 THE GREAT DEPRESSION
    These were the worst of times and, as they led into WW II,
    they got worse. Trade slumped more than 60%. Worldwide
    Industrial production falls by more than 40% and more
    than 12 million people are out of work. People losing
    homes, farms and dignity as banks close. Soup lines
    and 'shanty towns' spring up everywhere

1932 Franklin Delano Roosevelt became President

1933 Adolph Hitler takes power as leader of the extreme
    right- wing Nazi Party

1935 The dependable Douglas DC-3 aircraft becomes
    the work-horse of aviation

1934 Stalin begins his purge in Russia

1936 Jesse Owens is snubbed by Hitler after winning
    4 gold medals at the Olympics

1937 Elizabeth Wall graduates high school

Stalin

Hitler & Mussolini

Elizabeth

**President
Franklin
Delano
Roosevelt**

FDR whistlestop

**Winston
Churchill**

Class of 1937
Elizabeth: forth from left, front row
Arthur J. Roberts: first on left, top row

THE

Fifty-Ninth Annual

Commencement

OF THE

Faribault High School

June 6-11
Nineteen Hundred and Thirty-seven

"TYPICAL" TEEN

It was during my high school years that the world began to get bigger for me as we started learning more about the grown-up world. Until then we didn't know much about gangsters, the Era they called 'The Roaring Twenties' (except how to dance the Charleston and wanting to wear short, flair skirts like the 'flappers'), gambling or Prohibition. Really, we had no way to find out. We had no radio until about 1935 and no telephone until 1939, but we never missed these 'luxuries' until we had them. Funny how that works, isn't it?

The Wall Girls: (l. to r.) Cecelia, Elizabeth, Julia, Catherine & Mary.

Some of the best of times were those occasions when the parlor rug would be rolled back, and Johnnie Birch and our cousins Ed and John Gruber would become the band with fiddles, harmonicas and guitars. Daddy would call the squares and we would all dance until we dropped. Oh, I do miss those times. Such innocence, such closeness and such happiness. We would eat and sing and dance, dance, dance. We were isolated from all the problems of the outside world and very secure in our own little world.

It is curious but back then we danced and called it fun and today dancing is called aerobics and is good for your cardio-vascular system. We certainly have come such a long, long way. I only hope there is as much love, caring and genuine happiness in this 'dot.com' world for the children.

Have I mentioned how content, happy-go-lucky and well cared for we were during these years? I thank God every day for all the many blessings He has showered upon me and mine throughout my 82 years and I do plan on thanking Him for quite some time to come.

George

We didn't have a car at home until my brother George bought a Model A Ford in 1935. I remember that my first trip in a car was with my sister Catherine that very same year. I was turning 'sweet 16' and what a thrill. We drove to her house in St. Paul and then went to the State Fair with some relatives and friends. Not long after this major acquisition of an automobile, my sister Mary drove her friend, Catherine Lynch, to visit the McInerny's in Millbrook, South Dakota and I tagged along. About all I can recall from this adventure is a very long, hot and dusty drive. But the McInerny's lived on a farm and owned a pony that I could ride guaranteeing me a most memorable summer. The trip proved a great success because I enjoyed many pony rides and Catherine Lynch later married John McInerny.

Our Model A

The old neighborhood was alive with so many good friends and relatives. Bill Miller owned the grocery store across the street from us and he was always so kind to us. His oldest child was John followed by Jane who was my sister Mary's age and Wm. "Bing" was in my class. We still see each other around town after all these many years and have attended many a class reunion. Bing still calls me 'Lizzy', a terrible habit he picked up when were young because he knew I hated it. He and my brother George were good friends and, being industrious as only they could be, besides making the family root beer they had a sideline making wheat wine in the basement   At least until the day mother found out. Uncle John stopped by one very hot afternoon for a chat, and mother asked George to fetch his uncle a glass of root beer. Well, George thinking he is going to slip Uncle John a 'wee taste' of the 'spirit' without mother ever finding out, you know, a secret man-to-man understanding. Well I'll tell you, Uncle John took one long drink from that glass and gasps,

Elizabeth, Bing Mary and Pete

"Root beer hell! That's pure moon!" This episode rather dampened George and Bing's great talent for fermenting wheat.

After graduating high school, I went to work at the Rice County Court House in the Register of Deeds office. I made about $50.00 a month and would give it to my mother to help keep up the house. She would allow me 4 or 5 dollars spending money for the month and that was plenty. I lived at home, ate at home and with three older sisters I had all the clothes I needed. With my bicycle as transportation there was no need for gasoline. I thought this was really the life! I had some money in my pocket, friends at every turn, a good job and the means to travel all about town.

Off to work

There was this fellow, Frank Matejeck, who was a member of the local Sky Club and visited the Court House office on a regular basis. He was always talking about his flying experiences. Oh, I loved to hear those stories and he knew I was really interested. One day he asked, "Miss Wall, how would you like to go for an airplane ride?" "Would I, would I! Why I'd love to go for an airplane ride!" I must have appeared rather keen on the idea, because that next Saturday, I was at our little 'airport' and climbing into the seat of a 65hp Piper Cub.

13

(I don't mean to down play our airport at all, but it was really just a cleared cornfield or pasture. When taking off east or west, you had to fly either just over or just under the telephone wires.) Al Voegel, a friend of Frank's, was my pilot that day and off we went into the wild, blue yonder. Ohh... Ahh...I thought I had died and gone to heaven!

After flying straight and level for a little while making some easy turns and banks, he asked if I would like to try some aerobatics. Well, not knowing exactly what they were, I said sure. He took us up to about 3000 ft, stalled the plane and we went into a spin.

65 hp Piper Cub

Down and down we spiraled. After leveling out, he looked back to see if I was using the brown bag which I wasn't, and I smiled, held up one finger and asked, "One more time?" So up we went again, and again and yet again. After about 10 'one more times', he landed that plane, excused himself for a moment (I thought he looked a little green) and when he returned he said to me, "Miss Wall, whatever else you do in your life, you have to learn how to fly. I have made every newcomer who flies with me sick doing those stunts. You're the only one who has ever made me sick!" And so began my 'love at first flight.' After that exhilarating flight, I could not get out to the airport often enough, even though it was about 4 miles south of town and my only transportation was my bicycle. I would sweep out the office, do their bookwork, mow the lawn, tally the time to be billed for flying the plane, wash the planes, anything at all to get chances at more airplane rides.

Because there was a war being fought, many airfields were closed so their gasoline could be rationed where needed. But, because we had a Civil Air Patrol unit and were supposed to protect our borders, our field remained open. Oh how lucky for me. One thing about 'protecting the borders' was all we had to fly was a 65hp Piper Cub. Our 'bombs' were sacks of flour that we would practice dropping on a big X we had painted on the ground. God help our borders! Three of my sisters, Mary, Julia and Cecelia, also joined the Civil Air Patrol and we had so many wonderful outings and thrilling rides together. There was also the Sky Club at the airport consisting of 15 local men.

C.A.P. uniform

14

One day, one of the Sky Clubber's enlisted in the Army Air Corps and the Sky Club asked if I would like to become number 15.

I was so excited I was beside myself and almost forgot to ask about the requirements. "Well Betty, all you need is $100.00." "A hundred dollars, a hundred dollars! Where am I ever going to get a hundred dollars?" "Miss Wall, where there is a will." It proved just as true then as it is now, that flying is not just for the wealthy; it's for anyone with the will to fly. I heard somewhere that banks loaned money so I mounted my bike and with great determination rode off to our local bank and marched in to see the president.

1940 Faribault Sky Club

I said, "Mr. Kaul, I need $100.00." He looked rather curious and asked, "Miss Wall, what do you need all this money for?" I answered, "I'm going to learn how to fly" and he said, "I have loaned money to women for college, travel, fur coats, houses and cars. But never for flying lessons and besides, women don't fly." Pointing at myself I said with conviction, "This one's going to." He took out the loan papers and asked, "And what do you have for collateral?" After he explained what collateral was I answered, "Well, I have my bicycle." You know, Mr. Kaul never said a word or broke a smile. He filled out the papers, I signed them, we shook hands and off I went on my bicycle with a hundred dollars in my pocket - the happiest girl in the whole wide world. I was so buoyant I might have floated back to the airport. Imagine, me in the Sky Club! I did learn years later that Mr. Kaul had co-signed my note HIMSELF! Try finding a banker like that today. He did know our family, and though we had little money, he knew we were honest, hard-working people. Having a good name is so very important.

Transportation & collateral

DATELINE

1937 Japan invades China and controls all of the coastline, including Nanking, the Capitol

1938 Germany flexes its muscle by threatening to invade Czechoslovakia

1939 "Gone With the Wind" premiers in Atlanta, Georgia and "The Hobbit" is published by J.R.R. Tokien

1939 Germany invades Czechoslovakia

And Still Flying

Pearl Harbor

Declaration of War

Tires rationed

Ration lines

Rationing with a smile

W.W. II 1939-1945

1940 World Population – 2.295 billion
1940 Rationing as policy became reality
1940 Earnest Hemingway writes "For Whom the Bell Tolls"
1941 December 7: Japan attacks Pearl Harbor
1941 December 7: U.S. declares war on Japan
1941 December 11: U.S. declares war on Germany and Italy

1941 Declaration of WAR. Americans unite and stand ready to defend their land. Americans from the soup lines and Americans from the dust bowl more than rose to the moment. Americans found themselves in command of such a burning energy to put things right with the world. An energy that surfaces when one is violated to the extreme. An energy that transforms ordinary men and women into a collective avenger of evil and protector of righteousness. An energy so essential to survive places that became their own brand of hell. The call of a Nation to extinguish this brand of barbarism and terror was answered en masse`. From where did this spirit of patriotism and intense dedication to the cause spring? From inner city Public Schools, from one-room country schools and from the fields and factories of the land. From the bakeries, banks and businesses. Men and women from every walk of life and every set of circumstance rallied together. But each of them came from the heart and soul of a free nation: America. The common threads weaving them together were a faith in God, belief in country, love of family, appreciation of friends, dedication to duty and respect for life. A generation that put forth a concerted effort above and beyond the call throughout this unfathomable horrible, magnificently heroic period; the likes of which may never have been seen before and, God willing, will never raise its ugly head again. Those still living and those who have passed beyond the offing, are the men and women who have influenced the lives of the men and women who are the mothers and fathers of our Future – The Children. A thank-you from this world can never equal the Supreme Sacrifice that carried so many to the other side and those veterans passing away at the rate of 1000 a day.

1942 The first nuclear reactor goes on line
1942 The Manhattan Project: explodes 3 atomic bombs
        in Los Alamos, N.M.
1942 With men enlisting, women are called upon to take
        over in factories, farms, Postal services, transportation
        and other necessary support positions
1943 Elizabeth Wall joins the W.A.S.P.'s

SWEETWATER & AVENGER FIELD

Not long after my first flight and becoming a member of the Sky
Club, I saw a notice on the bulletin board at the airport stating
that the Military was interested in women pilots who could
assume some of the duties the men pilots had been assigned
freeing them for combat overseas. It listed the requirements
as either having a private pilot license or 35 hours of flight time.
5'3' was the minimum height allowed and with a few extra pairs
of socks and lifters I passed that one. We had to pass a physical
examination and be of a 'mind' to serve our country in the
military. Well, I didn't wait around for a private license. I logged
my 35 hours of flight time and headed off to Sweetwater, TX.
My sister Mary and another girl from Faribault, Kay Murphy, were
also accepted into this women's flight program and we ventured
down to Avenger Field our training base in Texas. (By the way,
to this day I have never had a private license. I advanced from
student pilot to having a commercial rating.) There were over
25,000 applicants for this military duty, 1800 were accepted
and 1074 of us received our silver wings. Imagine, in all those
numbers, 15 girls were from Minnesota and 3 of us were from
Faribault, MN. a town with a population of 14,527.

**'Rosie the
Riveter'**

Kay Murphy and I did graduate and receive our silver wings but
my sister Mary, God love her, could not pull out of a spin and
was mustered out of the program. She was afraid she would spin
in on top of someone, hurting or killing them. This accident had
happened at Avenger and one of our girls was killed. Of course
we all knew about this incident and it had a different affect on
each of us. Mary was more than a good student and a very
careful pilot. She was very intelligent and excelled in all the
ground school courses and was a tremendous help to me in
passing the book studies but she could not pull out of a spin.

So, we find ourselves at Avenger Field where every experience
is a new experience.

Imagine, after flying out of a cornfield in a 65hp
Cub, to be stationed at a REAL military base.
I really had arrived in heaven. I do have to mention
that while it is true we were wild about flying these
planes, it was just as important, if not more so,
that we knew in our hearts that we were serving
our country as only and as best as we could.
The reality of the war coupled with the number
of people who wanted and expected us to fail,
made us work all the harder to succeed.

Elizabeth, Kay & Mary

Family portrait shortly before leaving for Texas

Enjoying the view

Avenger Field at Sweetwater, Texas

Main Gate

Elizabeth, Kay & Mary

Our Official Vehicle

It wasn't easy, but as the song says on the new CD, 'Marching Songs of the WASP', "We got the stuff, the right stuff" (written by Deanie Parrish, Class of 44-4, performed by her daughter, Nancy and produced by Wings Across America). And Amelia Earhart noted, "A girl must nowadays believe completely in herself as an individual. She must realize at the outset that a woman must do the same job better than a man to get as much credit for it."

When we first arrived at Sweetwater, we took the oath of the military and were under orders at all times. We lived in barracks, ate in a mess hall (the food wasn't too bad), did our calisthenics at 6 A.M. and had our own 'official' transportation - an old cattle truck. Believe me, you knew it was a cattle truck. They had cleaned it out pretty well and put boards down both sides to sit on, but it was still a cattle truck. Something I don't understand to this day is that after we were all in the 'bus', the door was locked from the outside. I don't know where or why they thought we might escape because all we wanted to do was to fly those planes. Some procedures can only be explained as just being a part of the military way. We were let out of the 'bus' upon arrival at our destination but it was still a curious practice.

18

We wore turbans on our heads so as not to distract the civilian, male instructors with our flowing hair and we marched everywhere we went, just like in my grade-school days. We wore whatever uniform issued to us even though these uniforms were hand-me-downs from the men. You can imagine what we must have looked like wearing a man's size 44. This took some creative designing and was really quite a trick, but we all learned to master the technique. Sometimes we would need suspenders to hold up the pants, extra socks to snug up the boots and pillows to sit on so we could reach the pedals of the plane.

Mess hall

Turbaned Fly Gals

But we didn't care what we looked like; just let us fly those planes. These were <u>our</u> true 'Zoot' suits and we wore them well.

Government issue flight suits

During the years the W.A.S.P.'s were activated we had no insurance coverage. The Military never made us an official wing of the Army Air Corps, so there was no Government coverage, and the private sector thought our job was too dangerous. I can't imagine why they thought being shot at with live ammunition was so dangerous. The saddest part of this snafu was that when one of our girls was killed in the line of duty, the girl's family received a telegram from the Government, and if the family could not afford to have the body sent home, we would take up a collection among us and one of us would escort the body home. But there was no flag for the coffin or star for the window letting people know that this was a veteran being laid to rest. It was as if we were not taken seriously, but how much more serious can you be than being willing to give your life for your country? People ask if we were afraid, but we were young and did not believe that anything bad could ever happen to us. Being fearless is part of the beauty of youth. It was on Aug. 5, 1943 that women pilots and trainees were officially designated as W.A.S.P.'s, Women Airforce Service Pilots. Prior to this, the women ferrying planes, mostly the P-47 Thunderbolt off the factory line, were known as W.A.F.S. (Women's Auxiliary Ferrying Squadron). These were the original W.A.S.P.'s. and to join the Ferrying Squadron at that time these women had to log 200 hours of flight time!

Staying in shape

Gen. "Hap" Arnold

Our organization succeeded primarily because of the dedicated efforts of Jacqueline Cochran, Director of Flying, General H. H. "Hap"Arnold, Chief of Staff of the U.S. Army Air Corps and the First Lady Eleanor Roosevelt. In my opinion, Jacqueline Cochran has done more for women in aviation than anyone else. Besides being the top rated woman flyer during this period with her speed and other records, she had the vision and strength to open doors for other women to do service for their country as pilots and had the energy, stamina and 'clout' to make it happen. She knew that

Jackie Cochran

Cheerleaders

0600 Physical Training

The Wishing Well

Winter Suits

The Snow Lady

women pilots could handle any airplane, carry out any given order, and carry it out with flare and successfully. This demonstration made the future for women in aviation more acceptable, less hampered and enjoyed by greater numbers of women. If you should have the chance to read Jacqueline's story, Please Do! You will not be disappointed. She was a girl with very little means, many forces against her and still she made it to the top.

General Arnold, the only airman to become a Five Star General, saw the necessity and feasibility of such a program for women pilots and was very supportive in 'making it happen' amidst the many opponents and doubters. What can one say about our First Lady Eleanor Roosevelt? If there was a reasonable opportunity to advance the cause of women in any field Eleanor was in support of it, and hers was a voice to be reckoned with.

The training period at Avenger Field was dramatically different from anything most of us had ever experienced. From the very beginning with Class 43-1 the W.A.S.P. program was graduating one class per month. Our uniforms were khaki slacks, a white blouse and a service-issued overseas cap. There were a few experiences, events and traditions that did help maintain some sense of normalcy and connection to home for us. We had a wishing well, yes with water in it, where we tossed in pennies (if we had them) before taking a check ride with an instructor or an examination at school for good luck.

After a solo flight in an aircraft, the initiate was ceremoniously tossed into the well, but we did pull her out again. Our mascot, the winged gremlin Fifinella, had been designed for us by Walt Disney, and was with us all the time. We kept her for luck, but if something bad should happen, we could always blame it on her and one of her mischievous moods.

Baptized

It snowed during the winter of 1943-'44, but coming from Minnesota, it was really only a dusting. But, there was enough snow to plaster a snow woman against the barracks, and you could tell it was a snow woman. There were monthly dances at one of the close-by cadet fields that we rarely missed, even though we were transported in our 'official vehicle'. Sometimes, my sister Julie would visit and I would dress her up in one of my uniforms and we would always have so much fun. The W.A.S.P.'s celebrated their first birthday on November 12, 1944 and, oh, what a party. The 'Avenger', newspaper for the W.A.S.P.'s, had a front-page article that summed up the festivities quite well.

20

Fifinella by
Walt Disney
Productions

"LOCAL OFFICIALS PAY TRIBUTE TO WASPS FOR SERVICE TO CITY

...and their party was complete with parade, brass bands, the Sweetwater Texas Defense Guard as escort, the world premier of the Paramount-Avenger Field film short, and a multi-layered cake of gigantic proportions."

Those were the days my friends.

Our training was split between ground school and flight school. It was bad enough not being a great student, but not being a great student early in the morning was really tough. I had no college education and my high school curriculum was primarily preparing me for secretarial work and domestic chores and duties. Our ground school studies included meteorology, Morse code (I sort of remembered the dahditdit dadit dadada dadadada from my Civil Air Patrol days), navigation, the theory of flight, aircraft design, physics (I thought physics was something

you took for a stomachache), engines and math. I struggled through this entire regimen, but with many dedicated hours of hard study, many prayers to every saint in heaven so I wouldn't miss one and the constant help and encouragement of my dear sister Mary, I did pass. The physical fitness calisthenics and close-order drills were a relaxing interlude compared to the demands of studies and tests in ground school.

Flying was an entirely different story. Flight School, and the thrill of flying. We were introduced to the Fairchild PT 19, a 175hp puddle-jumper with an open cockpit that was our primary trainer. Oh, how I could soar. After our 65hp Cub in Faribault I thought I had died and gone to heaven again. (People talk about the nine lives of a cat!) After going through the paces in the PT 19, we moved on to the BT 13. Now there was a fun plane! As a basic trainer, it had all the bells and whistles I had ever hoped for. It had a canopy and all the zip and thrust for aerobatics and stunts provided by a 450hp Pratt and Whitney power plant. My, my, heaven was getting better looking at every turn. I could do the aerobatics and cross-country missions without a hitch. We did many cross-country flights because we never knew if we would be attached to the ferry or the training command.

It was about this time that an old boyfriend of mine from Faribault, Ambrose Mariska, visited. He was a flying farmer who owned his own plane. Having business in Kansas City, he decided

An instructor

Ground School

Flight Operations

Charting Cross Country

Elizabeth & Instructor

21

Right at home

PT 19

BT 13

AT 6

to drop down to Avenger Field for a 'formal' visit. His first words were, "O.K. Betty, you've proven that you can fly all these planes and now its time to come home and marry me." Well, I thought about it and really, what was a girl supposed to do? The war would not last forever and I did miss my family and friends back home. It is true that he did have a plane and I had flown everything the air force had given us for training and he really did have that plane, and so I said yes. He said fine and to go pack up. I told him I could not possibly leave without submitting my resignation, (we were considered civil servants so we could retire with no repercussions), turn in all my equipment, and say good-bye to all my wonderful friends and to my planes. I told him I would meet him in Kansas City when all this was completed in about three days time. He said O.K. and he returned to K.C. I went into our commanding officer and said, "Miss Deaton, I'm going to resign." She said, "Why on earth would you want to resign?" I told her about the flying-farmer and his airplane as she examined my file and then she said, "You're doing so very well with your flying and you are passing your ground school, but if this is what you want, I wish you Godspeed and all the happiness in the world. But before you go, I would like you to have a ride in that plane." She pointed to an AT-6. I went out to the flight line, got into that plane, took off in that plane and put that plane through all the paces I knew. I landed that plane, called my boyfriend and said "I'm not coming home!" He said that if I didn't, he would go home and marry someone else. Well, he did go home and marry someone else, I stayed at Avenger Field and we both lived happily ever after.

Heaven was never like this before. The AT-6. The Texan. The plane I had a love affair with and no regrets. The AT-6, my favorite aircraft. What you could do in that plane. It was the most famous trainer during WW II and earned the nickname of the 'Pilot Maker'. It had a 550hp Pratt and Whitney engine, a canopy and retractable landing gear. As you may have guessed by now, I stayed to complete my training.

By now, word had spread to other military bases in the area and their cadets that women were flying 'their' airplanes over at Avenger Field. Because the military did not know what type of plane we could handle we got to fly all of them. During the years the W.A.S.P.'s were active, we flew every type of aircraft the military had. All 77 of them, up to and including the B-29.

We had all our training at one field: primary, basic and advanced. We were, are and will be the only all girl air base in the world and we were dubbed 'Cochran's Convent' by some of those thinking us too prudent. And yes we were, but more importantly, we could not make a mistake or we'd be washed out. The Russians and English did have women pilots at that time, but they used the same fields as the men. Even our boys did their primary training at one field, basic at another and advanced flying someplace else) As this word spread around the area, we started having many incidents of engine trouble, right over Avenger. Planes would run out of gas, right over Avenger. Pilots were getting lost, right over Avenger. Gas was in short supply or was some how mysteriously sucked right out of the plane, right over Avenger. Our airspace and field became so busy with all these 'emergencies', Avenger

Field was put "off limits" to all male pilots. I thought that not having unscheduled visits by all these male pilots was an absolute shame. Having all three phases of flight training at this one field, and graduating one class per month, you can imagine how busy our airstrip had become.

Between the years 1943-44, the W.A.S.P.'s did 89% of all the ferrying in our country and 85% of all the training. In 1944, W.A.S.P.'s ferried every P-47 off the factory line. With our girls already ferrying planes from plant to base or base-to-base, it became apparent that we needed our own uniform. It was not considered 'lady-like' for a woman to wear slacks in public in those days and the planes we flew had no room for suitcases. It was not all that unusual to be denied a seat in a restaurant, or on a bus, or a room in a hotel. We were also issued our own parachute that we carried with us at all times. Being suspect right away because of our attire, it did happen on occasion that we were accused of stealing Government Property by local authorities and detained. This was not only embarrassing but also most inconvenient. Being held required a call to the Military Police

Graduation

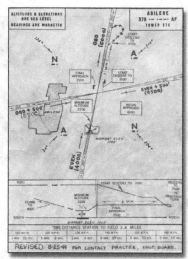

Cross Country Map

who then called the commanding officer of our home base who then ordered our immediate release because we were needed for transporting airplanes yesterday. This arrest was just one big hassle. I do have to say that most of the citizenry were pleasantly curious, most gracious hosts and more than helpful during these years. And so, uniforms were not only well deserved, but also necessary. During the course of my training at Sweetwater from August 9, 1943 to February 11,1944, Jacqueline Cochran designed our uniform and had it approved by Secretary of War, Henry L. Stimson. We were issued our Santiago Blue uniforms complete with beret the January before my graduation and our class had the distinct honor of debuting these 'new blues' at that ceremony. Other branches of the military have since adopted Santiago Blue as their colors and the Thunderbirds look so 'smart' in theirs today, but the W.A.S.P.'s introduced this color.

And finally came our graduation and I received my silver wings decked out in my Santiago Blues. Oh, my beautiful silver wings. If you ever see pilot wings with a diamond in the middle, know that they belong to a W.A.S.P. and they are a one of a kind. After graduating and receiving our new orders we had our first leave since beginning our training way back in August, a lifetime ago. As far as duty stations went, again, because no one was sure what craft we could fly, we were asked what command we preferred to join and usually were granted our wish. I love to fly pursuits, so I opted for the training command at Las Vegas Army Airfield. When I arrived back in Faribault in my Santiago Blue uniform, my officers' coat, beret, silk scarf and my silver wings; if you didn't think I was a hot pilot, all you had to do was ask. It was wonderful seeing my family and all my friends, but I was aching to get back to my duty and my love, flying planes. Las Vegas here I come! (An aside on my officers coat. Though I never had the opportunity to attend college, my coat ventured off to higher education with each of my children their freshman year at their various schools. Times change, but my uniform is forever in style.)

Liz in officers coat

LAS VEGAS

Official photo announcing our Las Vegas arrival

When we arrived at Las Vegas in February of 1944, it was not generally known that there were women pilots flying military aircraft, so you can imagine the reception the eight of us W.A.S.P.'s received. The others were: Ruth Jones, Ida Carter, Jeanette Jenkins, Gwen Crosby, Madelyn Taylor, Margaret Harper and Marie Mountain.

One quick story about Marie. She spoke extremely correct English, was most prim and proper and never, ever got flustered. On a training mission with an instructor as he rolled the craft, Marie's seat belt broke and she fell out of the airplane! She did have her parachute on, and thank God landed safely. We were all certain she would come undone after this event and make a wild scene. When she returned to the ready room, expecting some degree of ranting or at least highly stimulated excitement, we asked her what had happened and how she felt. After taking a controlled breath she calmly and matter of factly explained as she looked us over one at a time, "When I realized I had left the aircraft, I simply counted to ten and pulled the cord." Oh, we could have killed her ourselves.

A real pilot

That women were flying military aircraft did raise a couple of eyebrows. The men pilots considered themselves a unique fraternity among the many branches of military service and with reason. When women took over the controls of these bombers and fighter aircraft, some of the men were curious, others indignant. We simply settled in, took our orders and flew our missions with flare – determined to excel amid all this overly concerned observation, brouhaha, close scrutiny, and "I bet ya can't "attitude". Even the Officers initially had their doubts. But not for long. After a few missions, most men on the field at least accepted our existence if not our competence.

A few of our jobs at Vegas were training gunners on the ground and in the air. We would tow long muslin sleeves behind a B-26 and be shot at with LIVE ammunition by diving fighters. Each fighter pilot had a different colored bullet, so the instructors could tell which pilots were scoring hits. And to think this was practice for them! At least the colored bullets let us know who was putting the holes in our planes and not in the targets. Our shot-up 'sleeves' had their own sort of aesthetic appeal so we used them as curtains in our quarters to help keep the sand out. Oh, all that sand everywhere. Nothing like the practical woman's touch to spruce things up and make life more bearable.

Instructor, Marie Mountain in cockpit and Madeline Hill

At other times, we would dive in at the bombers in pursuit planes and the bomber crew would shoot at us with camera guns this time, thank God. It was unnerving watching these films. When you were hit, you could almost imagine yourself being shot out of the air! Because we were women, and again no one being certain what planes we could fly, or what missions we could handle, we were checked out in every plane on the flight line.

B-26

Towing target

Diving in on B-17's

Liz and Liz Watson

How lucky for us. If a man was checked out in pursuits he stayed inpursuits. If his plane were a bomber, he stayed with bombers and so on. Because I was checked out in pursuits and bombers I sometimes flew as co-pilot on these training flights. To be a co-pilot in a B-17 was a real treat! I also was co-pilot in the B-26 called "The Widow Maker" because of its short wingspan it had a high accident rate. It could be tricky on take-off and landing but once you got her in the air could she maneuver!

And then, on one particular day I was called into Flight Operations and given the mission of diving in on an infantry division over at Indian Wells with an AT-6, my favorite plane of all. I should mention again that there were only eight of us "lady" pilots stationed at Las Vegas. Our very existence not generally known and our flying missions not as yet part of the usual routine. My orders this day were to dive in at an infantry troop hunkered down in a bunker and let them sight in on me with anti-aircraft film-loaded machine guns and shoot me. I signed an order not to fly below 500 feet, complete the diving run, fuel up and return to base. I thought the form said 50 feet and I was not given specific approach directions for my strafing run. From the distance, I could see these boys in their bunker facing north

searching the sky for the "intruder." This seemed much too easy, and knowing this was combat training, I took the initiative to circle to the south and approach from the rear on a surprise attack. Just as I was over the bunker, (and I mean JUST over their bunker) I changed the prop pitch on my AT-6 and ohh...what a lovely sound! I looked back as I passed and every one of those boys had hit the deck! I had a little chuckle, circled again and dove at them from the North. I could almost hear those guns a 'blazing'.

Thank God their ammunition was FILM! After the run, I landed for fuel and a critique on my mission. I'm a pilot, but I'm a woman pilot, so before I jumped from the cockpit, I took my comb and lipstick from my leg pocket, 'gussied' up a bit and lit to the wing. As I was preparing to fuel-up, a lieutenant came boiling up to my plane fuming, pacing and mumbling. He looked in the cockpit, around the plane and then blustered up to me and demanded to know where the pilot was that flew that last mission. I told him that I was his pilot and somehow I don't think he said what he had planned on saying. In a toned down rage he went on and on about how that mission was supposed to play out, how I had scared the 'bejeepers' out of his boys (and I'm sure him too) and that he was going to report me. Being somewhat surprised -but not really- I asked him where 'his' boys were going from here?

He said, "they are going overseas to combat and I want them to live to get there!" Thinking fast on my feet, I said, "Well do you think the enemy is just going to coast in on them, wiggle their wings and say "come on fellas, shoot me down?" "
To this he had no other reply than "humph" and stomped off in a huff. As it turned out his boys had the highest gunnery marks to date and this type of 'surprise' attack actually became part of the regular training exercise. He never did report me and later on we even became friends.

A woman pilot

Even though the effects of G-force were not totally understood at this time, it was a standing order that no one, man or women, was to fly more than four hours a day. But, as I was young, healthy and felt certain that

nothing could happen to me, after flying my own missions, I would hang around the ready room and wait for the inevitable. You know, some of those boys returning from town (Las Vegas) sometimes didn't look so good. They looked a bit green, like that fellow who gave me my first ride. They would struggle into a plane and start sucking up oxygen. I'd ask them if they wanted me to fly their mission and they usually said "O.K." They'd go into flight operations, sign their name on the manifest and then tell me what the mission was. They'd go off to bed, and I'd go off for the sky. If there ever had been a problem on that mission, someone would have sure been in for a surprise learning it wasn't a John Doe in that plane after all but a Jane Doe.

Having done this for apparently too long, one morning I could not get out of bed. I simply could not. I didn't feel sick, but I had zero energy and couldn't move, could not lift arm or leg. The other girls knowing that if I didn't get up to fly something was definitely wrong with me. I needed medical attention. They literally carried me to the flight surgeon who gave me a thorough examination. After determining there was nothing physically wrong with me, his diagnosis was explained as, "Miss? You're perfectly healthy, so you must be pregnant." I looked at him in utter surprise and indignantly answered, "I can't be pregnant because I'm not even married!" As he chuckled at that, but knew it to be true, it was decided I was suffering from flight-fatigue and given leave to recuperate. After a week of rest at home in Faribault, I shipped out to Orlando, FL. for two weeks at an Officer Tactical Course.

Elizabeth — You really are an ace in every way —
Love, Charlene Creger,
WASP "Lost last class" 44-10

It was a mandatory course and did extend my rest period from flying. Among other useful information, we learned military protocol, the ranking system and how to eat the cuisine of tropical islands: my first, only and hope-to-be-forgotten introduction to snake. I don't know if I could ever be that hungry. But really, snake wasn't too bad.

Rest and Relaxation at Jackie Cochran's ranch

By now I only wanted to get back to my duties and my planes. When I returned, I did settle into a more 'conventional' routine. I still hung around the flight line, but only to be close to the action. However, one day Lt. Marshall needed someone to fly a mission in a P-39. What a plane. This was a low winged Bell Aircobra. It had a tricycle landing gear; the engine was behind you, the crankshaft was between your legs and the propeller was in front of your nose. An Allison, 12-cylinder power plant, with speeds up to 330 mph at 5000 ft. provided more power than I had yet experienced. Did he ever find his someone! He asked if I thought I could handle it because it was a very 'hot' plane and I said "sure". The only thing I was concerned about was landing, because I had only flown 'tail-draggers' up until now. There were no flight simulators in those days, so if you were going to fly something you just got in and flew. Lt. Marshall said not to worry because he would talk me down on the radio. This is my kind of day! Off I go, and I mean GO! The speed, the maneuverability, the joy! After completing my mission I was checking in with Marshall for landing instructions and don't 'cha' know, my radio went dead. Now here's a fine how-do-you-do. Think fast Betty, this might be a test.

Barbara Erickson is the 1st WASP to receive the Air Medal for Meritorious Achievment as a pilot for logging four 2000 mile deliveries of three different types of aircraft in 5 days of actual flying time.

Having had some excellent training in my career I put the bird through some stalls to get some feel for the attitude the plane might have while landing. After a series of these when I felt comfortable, I circled for my final approach. Lt. Marshall must have announced that there was a wild woman up there coming in for a landing in a P-39, a plane she had never flown before and to dispatch the crash squad. As I'm circling, I look down and see fire trucks, an ambulance and other assorted emergency vehicles rushing to the scene with lights a-flashing. This only intensified my determination to make the perfect landing. Being the good pilot I am, I touched down at the very beginning of the runway. I'm clipping along, I'm clipping along, and along and along. He wasn't kidding that this was a 'HOT' aircraft! I came to halt at the very end of the runway and I saw a jeep screaming after me. As I come to a stop and the jeep pulled up next to my plane, Marshall jumped out of his vehicle and is all flustered.

P-39

Before he had a chance to say anything I asked, "How'd ya like my landing Marshall?" He quips, "Hell of a good landing Wall, but why didn't you use your flaps?" There may have been some other 'red-faced' moments during my flying career but we won't go into them.

Soon after this outing, I heard Las Vegas needed an instrument instructor so I applied for the job, was accepted and returned to Sweetwater for further instruction. It was like old home week being back at Avenger Field, only better. So many fond memories from not so long ago of modest means, special friends and simple pleasures. I studied hard, was certified and returned to Las Vegas as an instructor. Instrument flying was taught by putting a black hood over the trainee's seat. Pilots had to trust their instruments totally, no matter what his instincts, brain, feelings or 'guts' told him. You can become completely disoriented while flying in the dark: you could be screaming down toward the deck when you think you're flying straight and level. Along came one of my first students just a-dragging his heels. Here I am, all 5'3" of me in all my gear plus some pillows. And here is strapping 6'3" Jim Loosen with his parachute and a doomed look on his face straggling behind. I turned to him and said, "You don't want to fly with me, do you Jim?" He said, "No". I asked, "Are you afraid to fly with me, Jim?" He said, "Yes." Even though he was a very good pilot and knew that at least I was a pilot, he had his many reservations. Then I told him about the plan was. He was to take off and level off at 3000 ft., but when I wiggled the stick I wanted control of that plane. All went according to plan. When I got control, I put that bird through maneuvers I didn't even know I knew. I racked it to the limit and then some. After I thought I had made my point, we landed and I asked Jim that regardless of what position he got us into from under that hood, didn't he really believe that I could pull us out of it? He had to agree and we went on with our training. He proved to be one of my best students and I had very little trouble with anyone else not wanting to fly with me. Jim and I are still friends to this day.

I remember how big the world was getting for me back in high school by listening to a radio and making a phone call. Well here is a true story reminding me how small the world is getting today. Some friends of mine from Faribault, Stu and Lillian Thibodeau, were on a bus trip from the Phoenix area to Laughlin, NV to enjoy one of those 'sporting' days. On the bus as people are getting acquainted Stu is overheard saying he was from Faribault, MN. A fellow a few rows back on the bus said that he knew a person from Faribault named Betty Wall. Would you believe it? It was Jim Loosen!

Instrument training hood

Atomic bomb blast

Wars end

DATELINE

1944 W.A.S.P.'s deliver every P-47 Thunderbolt that comes off the Republic Aviation Factory Line

1944 Soldiers begin returning to the States as reinforcements arrive overseas

1944 First long-range guided missile is launched

1944 W.A.S.P.'s are deactivated

1945 The atomic bomb is tested

1945 May: W.W. II ends in Europe

1945 August: W.W. II ends in Asia

1945 More than 50 million people died worldwide died as a result of WW II. More civilians than soldiers lost their lives

1946 First computer goes on line

1946 War Crimes trials begin

1946 United Nations comes into being

Churchill, FDR & Stalin at Yalta

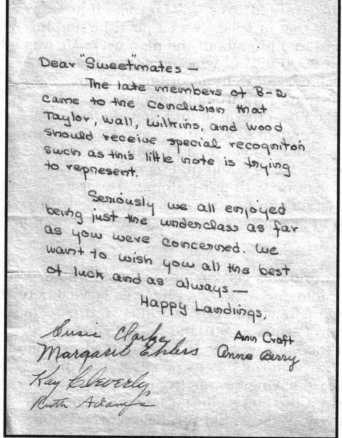

Dear "Sweetmates" —

The late members of B-2 came to the conclusion that Taylor, Wall, Wilkins, and Wood should receive special recognition such as this little note is trying to represent.

Seriously we all enjoyed being just the underclass as far as you were concerned. We want to wish you all the best of luck and as always —

Happy Landings,

Susie Clarke   Ann Croft
Margaret Ehlers   Anne Berry
Kay Cleverly
Ruth Adams

Class 44-1 appreciated by underclass women

DEACTIVATION & READJUSTMENT

These years in my life proved to be the time of my life. During such a drastic period of World War, these days seemed to good to be true. If heaven wasn't any better than this, I didn't want to go there anymore. This may seem to be a selfish and unwarranted statement, but what other circumstances would allow women to pilot these military planes? The answer is none. However, it did prove too good to last. On June 22, 1944, House Resolution 4219 terminated the training program for women pilots at Avenger Field. Accepting new trainees would end on June 30, 1944. The government wasted no time implementing this Bill and on December 20, 1944 the W.A.S.P. program, the Women Airforce Service Pilots, the branch of service we girls had grown to know as home and dearly loved was de-activated. What a crushing blow! After flying airplanes with four engines powered with 1200hp each, we were told to go home and lead normal lives. Would it be possible? We did understand that men pilots had returned from overseas and needed flight time to earn their pay, but what about us?

The Las Vegas Fly Girls last supper.

We realized we were fortunate to have had the airtime we did, but to be dismissed as 'second-stringers' did not sit well with us. As you can well understand, the 65hp Piper Cub did not excite me anymore. We were all devastated, disappointed and lost. We volunteered to fly these military planes without pay but the powers-that-be nay-sayed that offer. What were we to do? I just couldn't go back to secretarial work and I wasn't ready for the kitchen and a family. However, that was the way it was in 1944

They Clip Our Wings

and we accepted our lot without public fury or demonstrations. We were women of quiet dignity and inner turmoil: hurt but not defeated. We were not looking for special treatment; only the opportunity to do the job for which we were well trained and worked with great diligence to perform expertly. Instead, we were ushered back to our barracks, packed up our kit, grabbed our grip and found our own way home. We would have flown those planes for nothing if they had let us. We were offered other designations in the Army Air Corps, but flying was not an option.

Reviewing my resume`, I realized I was quite an accomplished pilot. I had earned a commercial license, a four-engine rating, instrument instructors' certificate and was even qualified with a seaplane rating by Stanley Sikora, a good friend and good fellow from Chicago. Why, I would fly for Northwest Airlines! I donned my finest 'off to interview' dress, gathered up my portfolio, put on a 'show of great confidence face' and went off to the NW Airlines offices, certain to be employed. I presented my resume`, answered some questions and was told I had a most impressive list of accomplishments. Then it was made perfectly clear that women did not fly commercially but I could be welcomed in their front office. Well, I told them what they could do with their front office and left the building a very dejected woman. This just wasn't fair, but that's the way it was back in 1944. (I didn't know at that time, but my day would come with the people at N.W.A. many years later)

Wanting to stay high

After that rejection, but wanting so desperately to stay involved with flying, I went to Air Traffic Control School in Kansas City with Ruth Story, a friend of mine from back home. We were certified and as I went off to Grand Island, Nebraska to an air traffic control weather station; my friend went off to Omaha and the airport tower as a flight controller. I was then sent to North Platte, Nebraska and, oh what a sad place that was!

Air Traffic School, Kansas City, MO

The beginning of the end for this kind of work started in Rawlings, Wyoming and the Sinclair Radio Station. Being the rookie, and a women rookie at that, the good old boys decided that I should break in on the night shift when there wasn't much action other than their card games and my taking the hourly readings: ceiling, temperature, precipitation, visibility, wind velocity and barometric pressure - out in the middle of a desolate nowhere. There was a shack, and I mean a shack, but the weather station itself stood about 60ft. off to be away from the light. Hah! What light? I had to carry a big stick to literally shoo the snakes and rats away. I was so lonesome, sad and depressed. I have always been around people, good people, and I just couldn't handle this isolated outpost. I handed in my resignation, bought a train ticket and went to visit my sister Julia in Los Angeles. It took me a while to accept the fact that I was no longer involved with the profession I so loved. After enough pouting and some insistence from Julia that I get off my duff and DO something. I began looking for gainful employment.

Rawlings, Wy.

I tried the office routine again and just couldn't sit still. I became an exercise instructor but didn't like the repetition. Class after class, the same old routine. I even became an archery instructor for the Hollywood starlets but couldn't stay focused. I worked in

Mama

the cashier's office at Firestone, hoping for a chance to fly their sponsored plane in the cross-country race. Again the man won out. Within these three years I held no less than fifteen different jobs. I was not very stable. I was a wreck and decided it was time to throw in the towel, bite the bullet, so to speak, and return to Faribault, MN; to a place I knew and I thought knew me. It should be easier getting into a regular schedule where I had done it before and where my adventure had begun. Besides mama was ill.

Archery instructor

DATELINE

1947 Elizabeth Wall marries Arthur Roberts
1948 First long-playing record (LP) is produced
1948 First Microwave oven introduced but not
      available in homes until 1955
1948 Post-War Problems
    • Goods and housing are in short supply
    • Rationing continued
    • Some women not content with "back to the kitchen"
    concept after being in the work force during war
1948 The first Credit Card is issued
1951 Peaceful uses for atomic energy are explored
1952 First jetliner, the 48 passenger De Havilland Comet I
      with four turbojet engines paved the way for regular
      transatlantic flight service
1953 First open heart surgery is performed
      by U.S. surgeon J. Gibbon
1953 Stalin dies
1954 First shopping mall opens in Northland, Michigan
1955 Disneyland opens
1955 The space-race is off and running
1955 Rosa Parks refusal to sit in the back
      of the bus sparked the Civil Rights Movement
      and desegregation
1956 First pacemaker implanted

Our Wedding Day

Liking the work-place

Rosa Parks

33

FAMILY

Golf the great relief

This was truly a bittersweet homecoming for me. I just couldn't muster up the enthusiasm or light-hearted, carefree attitude I once had taken for granted. It was as if I'd left the most important part of me somewhere else, but where, and would I ever find it again? Was I growing up and learning there were big bumps in the road? How disappointing and how unfair this all seemed. I did get my job back at the County Court House and tax time found me working with my sister Mary in Lucius Smiths' law office. I was going through all the right motions but I just wasn't feeling anything; I was numb.

Gradually, some degree of normalcy took hold as I saw more and more of my friends and went to dances many weekends in surrounding towns, and to parties and picnics in the summertime. My W.A.S.P. days seemed like an entirely different lifetime and besides, nobody was very interested in my stories anyway. Maybe it wasn't such a big deal after all. We had done our patriotic duty like everyone else. The war was over and it was high time to get on with the business of a peacetime life. It was becoming easier accepting this day-to-day life and my secret memories were so alive that they carried me through my sadness and my difficulties. Nothing seemed very important and yet, somehow, this life with family and friends in a peacetime setting was becoming the most important thing in the whole wide world. It was a sad parting as I put all my flying gear in the back of my closet and slowly put it all in the back of my mind.

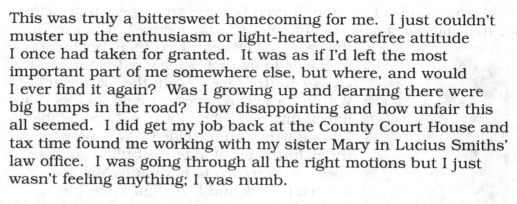

Elizabeth and Arthur Roberts

Life goes on and I was sick and tired of being sick and tired. And then it happened just like that. As I shifted attitudes and left the doldrums behind, right there in front of me was an old boy friend asking for an evening out. Before I had joined the W.A.S.P.s, he told me that if I enlisted I would no longer be his girl. He did come to visit me at Sweetwater while he was on leave from the South Pacific and, after seeing how happy I was, he reconsidered and told me to carry on. I remember our first date as if it were yesterday. We went to the Maison Ritz, a local nightclub, had a little bite to eat and our first dance was to "Blue Moon" by Frank Sinatra. I don't recall the conversation but I do recall being treated like a lady and realizing I was inwardly happy for the first time since leaving Las Vegas. We dated for a while and I thought I might finally be ready for the altar, the kitchen and a family.

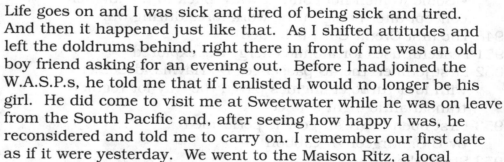

Arthur Roberts asked me to marry him during the summer of '47 and we were married on December 27, 1947. At first we stayed with my mother and sister while he and Rollie Hoban finished building our house on the east side of town about two

Wedding Party

34

and half miles away. We had our first son, Arthur, with us by the time we moved into our rather compact but cozy two bedroom home. In all, we had five children in 5 years. We were a close family and with the seven of us in a two bed-roomer, well, we got even closer. So close sometimes that we got under each others' skin. But wasn't this the American way? With my husband, all the babies and my wonderful friends and their children living in a safe enclosed neighborhood, each helping the other, and, even with all the kids in that one block area (about 25 very close in age) finding time for a weekly game of bridge. We had a roof over our heads, food to eat and friends to enjoy. Memories of my own childhood surfaced often. I did go visit my mother at times and always took my little ones. I had a baby carriage that curiously enough managed to accommodate three of them while two clung to the sides. I was healthy and gave little thought to the two-mile hike. Try to imagine packing gear for five kids, two still in diapers for a two-mile trek across town. Sometimes we would stop for a picnic along the way and must have been quite a sight. By this time in my life I was too busy and too tired to think about my W.A.S.P. life and I was happier than I had ever thought possible. At some point during the day, mother would watch the kids and I'd go grocery shopping at the Piggly-Wiggly Store around the corner. When Art finished work he would come pick us up with our weeks' worth of groceries and drive the lot of us to home sweet home. These were the days my friends.

Arthur jr. 1948

During the war, Arthur had been stationed in the South Pacific attached to the 455th Service Squadron with the US Army Air Force. He must have endured some dark times and weathered some horrendous storms because he never discussed those years of his life with me. I could not carry on about my service career with him because it was the difference between night and day. He asked me to postpone any flying until the kids were grown, and that request I could certainly understand. I couldn't imagine him with our five 'little angels' on his hands without my help so I respected his wishes as best I could. There were a few occasions when my friend Rita Orr would invite me along on excursions or some other friend would ask me up for a sea-plane ride or a Poker Run outing. These Poker Runs were always such fun. A group of planes would take off and fly to five neighboring town airports drawing a card from a deck. Whoever returned to 'home field' with the best poker hand would win the 'kitty'.

S/SGT
Arthur J. Roberts

It seemed we were always too busy even to get tired! Just as we dozed off, one of the children would begin to cry, need to be changed or want a glass of water. There was always at least one in diapers and formula for all to be heated. My mother thought I was overly conscientious regarding some of these motherly chores like sterilizing the diapers in a big old wash tub —no washing machine- drying them on our solar powered

And then there
were four

35

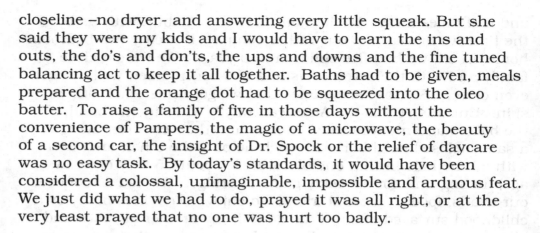

closeline –no dryer- and answering every little squeak. But she said they were my kids and I would have to learn the ins and outs, the do's and don'ts, the ups and downs and the fine tuned balancing act to keep it all together. Baths had to be given, meals prepared and the orange dot had to be squeezed into the oleo batter. To raise a family of five in those days without the convenience of Pampers, the magic of a microwave, the beauty of a second car, the insight of Dr. Spock or the relief of daycare was no easy task. By today's standards, it would have been considered a colossal, unimaginable, impossible and arduous feat. We just did what we had to do, prayed it was all right, or at the very least prayed that no one was hurt too badly.

Actually, raising children was a lot like flying airplanes, trial and hopefully not too much error. How did we survive without parenting classes, experts in child rearing or ballet classes? Well, we were never late for class, those experts didn't confuse us, and we didn't pay for something that, for most "kids", is just a passing fad. We lived in the hard working, make ends meet, black and white world of "Ozzie and Harriet", "Ed Sullivan", "Father Knows Best", "Bonanza" and "Wagon Train". If we did have a problem, we relied on our families, our very close friends, or if it was really serious, our parish priest. Neighborhoods seemed more closely knit, more like extended families, and you could always count on a hand when needed, even if only to be the fourth for a bridge game or to prepare an extra bowl of Jell-O.

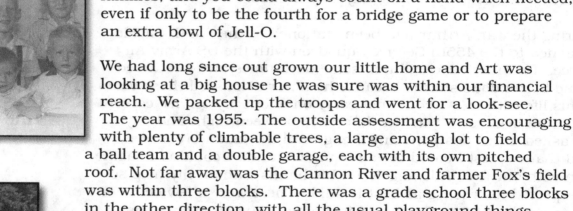

We had long since out grown our little home and Art was looking at a big house he was sure was within our financial reach. We packed up the troops and went for a look-see. The year was 1955. The outside assessment was encouraging with plenty of climbable trees, a large enough lot to field a ball team and a double garage, each with its own pitched roof. Not far away was the Cannon River and farmer Fox's field was within three blocks. There was a grade school three blocks in the other direction, with all the usual playground things, and an ice skating rink in the winter. My goodness, the hours of playtime away from home my warriors could enjoy. A definite win, win. Can we tour the inside? I could sense a measure of apprehension from Art as we entered the abode. The front door had a beautifully etched scene of deer grazing in a glen and right inside was the great staircase with splendid banisters (would require weekly dusting), the living room off to the left had two different entrances (convenient for something and, as it turned out, a few years later Art's father came to live with us and moved into this room having this entrance offering him some privacy and independence.)

Art and his father

The bathroom off the downstairs bedroom was handy but only had a stool and sink. And then there was the kitchen. It actually had a hand pump to draw up the water! The only cooking appliance was a gas jet pickling burner.

The basement was dark and dank (but the kids loved it 'cause it was like a dungeon right out of Frankenstein) the rooms were roomy and could be finished off nicely. The furnace was of the over-grown octopus style, and couldn't be very efficient. But gas was 'penny cheap' according to Redi-Kilowat so we might still be at the flip of a coin stage on whether or not to buy. Let's check out the upstairs, the kid's domain. A large closet was under the stairs and right at the top of the stairs was a generous storage area. There were three rooms that measured a very spacious 12'X12'. The boys were already staking out their space and my daughter was decorating a smaller room in her head. "Ah, where are the closets and the bath?" "Well you see, that's what puts it within our means. We'll just have to rough it till me and Rollie finish the remodeling. We'll do it after work till it's done." "You have got to be kidding. Do you remember your oldest of five children is only seven?" "We promise not to work him too hard the first few days. Anyway look at them. They've already moved in." "You have to promise to build me a brand new modern kitchen when you finish the bath and closets." "Sure dear." "You have to give me two nights out a week to visit my sisters." "O.K. dear." "And you have to help with the Saturday night basin baths." "Well, you know we could be working on the bathroom and the sooner we finish the bathroom, the sooner we no longer have to haul and heat water to fill the basin." He had me there, and so here we are and the stage is set for raising five children during the 50's and 60's in a big, old wonderful house.

Christmas with my sister Julia, her husband Bruce and our five children

It wasn't long before my 'nights out' were spent at P.T.A. meetings, Cancer Society volunteer work, American Legion Auxiliary activities, '99' meetings and other assorted groups and clubs. Art was superintendent of the gas department at Northern States Power Company, I was back on familiar ground at the County Court House, the children were in the hands of the nuns and God was in His heaven. All is well with the world. Eventually the bathroom and kitchen (with a dish washer!) were finished. The closet in the master bedroom downstairs turned out to be an antique armoire furnished by Art's parents, the double garage 'mysteriously' burned to the ground within a few years of our moving in and a snowball found its own way through the beautiful deer-grazing front window.

Liz in her office at the Court House

As I became committed to the demands and responsibilities of being wife and mother, my W.A.S.P. memories slowly faded to a quietly coveted treasure trove in the mist. Surfacing only during contact with one of my 'fly-buddies' or upon hearing a plane soaring past. Flying was the love of my youth, being married and raising children were the love of the here and now. Whenever life became too heavy, I could fancifully escape to those days of diving in on bombers and performing aerobatics in my beautiful war-birds and the sun would shine and rainbows welcomed me back to the joy of motherhood.

The great assortment of pets came and went, except for our Birch Coolie Buster, beagle extraordinaire and honorary family member who stayed with us for some eleven years. Fred Schuck, Buster's owner, brought his dog everywhere. The kids used to play with him at the Legion Club on Sunday mornings and after a month or so, Fred, saw that the dog was having as much fun as the little Roberts' so he passed over the pedigree papers and leash to Art saying the dog needed action, (and boy was he guaranteed that!) and more company than he could provide. Art told the kids that they could have him if they promised to take care of him; feeding, baths, walks and attention because he didn't have the time and besides, he wasn't overly keen on the idea.

But because Fred wants you to have him, we'll give it a trial. But Art wasn't fooling me. He loved that dog as much or more than any of us. I wonder just how much he really paid for our Buster?

We had a porch with roof running the length of the front of the house with a railing that was missing more than a few spokes. Another project that kept that house within our economic range. Why is that men have to engineer a little job for years and years before it gets into the rotation of maybe getting done? And then when they do tackle it there are all the stops for advice and hours at the Hardware store doing whatever men do in there. A part of his job with Northern States was to drive around the countryside and town checking on work in progress and looking for zones with possible leaks. He would drive by the homestead whenever he was in the neighborhood overseeing his estate and checking on what mischief the gang might be up to. One day as he's driving by he saw Buster hanging by his neck with his little feet barely touching the ground. He had jumped or fallen through one of the gaping holes where the spindles should have been. Art jumped from the car and freed Buster from his 'near-death' experience. Buster wouldn't have lasted much longer and Art was still shaking when he got home after work and told us about the near tragedy. How would he have felt if anything happened to our Buster, God forbid, because our porch was missing a few teeth? He would never have forgiven himself. He didn't say anything else, made a phone call and the next thing I heard was a lot of racket coming from the front of the house.

The kids would have gotten a rather intense verbal lashing considering the mood Art was in, so I hurried outside to quiet them down before their dad came out. What do I find? Not the brood making a ruckus, but Art and Rollie tearing down the porch! Sledge hammers, crow bars, other assorted wrecking tools and some kind of saw he said he had to have years before because it could do things no other saw could, (but this was the first time I'd seen it in action). They seemed to be on some sort of holy mission. Not speaking, focused totally on the next section of roof or support beam. Men possessed. Well into dusk, the banging stopped, a great quiet settled in and we all held our breath. Our neighbor, who also worked at NSP, came marching over. His babies must have just fallen off to sleep and he wasn't about to have them wake up because Art was into one of his "things". When he saw the expression on Art's face, I'm not sure what words were exchanged, but he picked some weapon of destruction and joined in the demolition. And he said he wasn't overly keen on Buster! It didn't take as long as most improvements to be enjoying a new entryway complete with a big, beautiful closet. Buster, you were the dog and what a good dog.

Liz and her mama

49er Days

There were the Cub and Boy Scouts, Brownies, ball games, paper routes, picnics and fishing vacations up north. Some vacation! Imagine packing for five kids to rough it in a cabin on some lonesome lake in the Great North Woods. We brought much of our own food and ate all the fish we could handle. We had fish for lunch and fish for supper and coolers of fish to bring home. Art loved these yearly get-aways and the children were in heaven with a lake outside the front door of our one room cabin and a boat at the dock. What could I say or do other than cook, clean and do the laundry.

We felt so secure on these excursions that we would leave our house door unlocked so one of our neighbors could come in and feed Buster. A terrible 'crime' of that time would have been spitting on the sidewalk. The policemen were our friends and the firemen would let the kids slide down the pole at the fire station. I understand the situations today with 'normal people' snapping, going off the deep end and committing some heinous crimes, and the reality of insurance claims against local departments and authorities have made this kind of openness and freedom not possible, but, as I have said before, these were different times.

Our dear sister Catherine

Living back in Faribault was all I remembered it to be as a child and it was wonderful. We had our cuts, scrapes, a broken bone or two, negotiations to be monitored between 'warring tribes' and prizes to be awarded to all my winners and now I was baking the bread and making donuts. Once we went camping with another family at one of our State Parks and I had two flat tires. My Boy Scouts said not to worry mom, so I didn't. We'd go walking in the rain and I'd explain weather systems. "What's the matter? Didn't your mother ever teach you to come in out of the rain?" "Heck no. She'd dress us up and take us out to play in it."

Arthur J. Roberts

To my thinking, it was a small town, Norman Rockwell kind of life. I had a good-looking, hard-working husband, a big old comfortable house, enough kids, a great dog and ample reasons to get out of the house on occasion: PTA, Cancer Society, the Legion Auxiliary, bridge parties and the like. As the kids grew, we did catch them sneaking out of the house in the middle of the night and they would explain that they were just keeping the town safe. Once, after Mike had returned from Viet Nam, Cece and I happened in on a keg party being hosted by my boys in my house. And somewhere along the line, that exquisitely etched window in the front door had mysteriously received a fatal blow from a snowball. I remember Art being furious but he finally said, "No sense crying over broken glass." We shrugged our shoulders, laughed a little and got on with the business at hand. We had learned to except a fact of life with kids, a little bit of good and a little bit of bad is normal. But all in all, they were good kids and I treasure every year I had them at home.

My sister Kay died in April of 1969 and Arthur died in October at the age of 50. I still had the two youngest at home and in high school, so at least I didn't have an empty nest. I began to reflect on our success at raising the kids. How do you know if you did a good job? Art always said I was too soft on them while he had to be the disciplinarian. I wouldn't really know until years later that the proof is in the pudding and apples don't fall too far from the tree.

My sister Mary died the following year and I just got sad. Life was so brief, so fragile. Some friends knew I needed a shot in the arm, so they talked me into running for public office, the Register of Deeds. I had worked at the Court House off and on (mostly on) for about 20 years and I had a good handle on its operations. My 'away' children came home from college bringing along friends and fraternity brothers to help canvass the town. We all had such a good lesson in the political process and I shared this experience with a great bunch of kids. The house was so full and abuzz with activity that my grieving soon faded. We put up a very good fight during the election, had a respectable showing and, even though I thought I was the better candidate, we lost by the narrowest of margins.

Our dear sister Mary

DATE LINE

1957 SPUTNIK 1 launched by USSR in October
1958 US launches its first satellite in January
      and the race for space has begun
1958 Boris Pasternak publishes "Dr. Zhivago"
1958 Charles de Gaulle comes out of retirement
      to head new government in France
1959 Bob Noyce prints first microchip beginning
      revolution in computers
1959 Fidel Castro overthrows President Batista
      in Cuba and takes control of the island
1960 Alfred Hitchcock releases his movie, "Psycho"
1961 Russian pilot, Yuri Gagarin, becomes first man in space
1961 Berlin Wall constructed between East and West Berlin
1962 First telecommunications satellite launched by U.S.
1962 Cuban Missile Crisis
1963 USSR Lt. Valentina Tereshkova
      became the first woman in space
1963 John F. Kennedy is assassinated
1964 Palestinian Liberation Organization (PLO)
      was founded in Jordan
1964 Dr. Martin Luther King comes to prominence
      as leader of the Civil Rights movement
1965 The "Sound of Music" becomes one of most popular
      and successful movie of all time

J.F.K.

Fidel Castro

41

Neil Armstrong

Neil's moon walk

VOTE FOR
ELIZABETH WALL ROBERTS
FOR
REGISTER OF DEEDS

Experienced - Qualified - Efficient
Native of Rice County, Familiar With
Problems & Aspirations of the Community.

Prepared, paid for and circulated by
Elizabeth Wall Roberts, Faribault, Minn.

1965-1973 VIET NAM WAR

1965 First pictures from Mars sent back to earth
from the US space probe, Marine 4
1966 First successful space link-up between 2 spacecrafts
1966 Chinese leader, Mao Zedong urges followers
to return to basic Communism
1966 India elects first woman Prime Minister Indira Gandhi
1967 The 'Greenhouse Effect' brought to light by scientists,
S. Manabe and R.T. Wetherald
1968 Dr. Martin Luther King is assassinated
1969 Arthur Roberts dies
1969 The music festival, Woodstock, attracts
more than 300,00 people
1969 First moon walk by US astronaut, Neil Armstrong
1970 USSR successfully lands lunar robot on the moon
1971 USSR successfully launches first space station
1971 Pocket calculator is developed
1971 The environmental activist organization,
Greenpeace, is formed
1972 Elizabeth employed by American Cancer Society

AMERICAN CANCER SOCIETY

I firmly believe that we all should keep looking for the silver lining through the dark clouds of life and that goodness and opportunity are ever present if only we will see. God was smiling on me on that November day that I lost the election because a door was opened for me to work for the American Cancer Society out of their headquarters in New York. I had been a volunteer for over fifteen years working on a survey investigating the effects of geography, life style, environment at home and work and family history of cancer on determining cancer causes.
My mother and sister had died of cancer and I wanted to do something. It was the spring of 1971 and I had two sons living in Boston. My friend, Mary Lou Pluemer, suggested we should get away for a while and visiting the boys was as good a reason as any. The next day, we packed our bags and were off for 'Beantown'. All was fine with the boys, at least as much as they shared with us, so Mary Lou and I went down to New York to tour the Headquarters of the American Cancer Society. We had been volunteers for this organization since 1958 collecting data for a study called the Laboratory of Life attempting to pinpoint cancer causing factors from evaluating diets, living habits, employment and environmental impacts from a cross section of citizens nationwide. This epidemiological survey, still in follow-up status today, has been crucial in further understanding the causes of cancer and advancing cancer research.

Upon arriving in New York, we contacted Alan Erickson, who had been our field representative in Minnesota and was now working out of the New York office. He arranged for us to meet Dr. E. Cuyler Hammond, President of the New York Academy of Science and Director of the Laboratory of Life study. We met with Dr. Hammond and his assistant Larry Garfinkel, biochemist and research analyst, in the Doctor's office. As we were making introductions and getting acquainted, the Doctor said thathe was a pilot and I mentioned that I had been a W.A.S.P. during the war. They were both genuinely interested and asked all the right questions. I could hardly believe that after all these years someone was interested in our organization. Dr. Hammond asked what I was doing for employment and I told him about the lost election. Then he said he had a position available for a statistical researcher that would involve traveling around the country to different State Capitols doing a follow-up study on the survey we had assisted with as volunteers. What do you think my answer was to that offer? Mary Lou and I went home, I called my children and told them what I was thinking of doing and they all said to go for it. I packed a bag and was on a plane back to New York City before I had a chance to change my mind.

**Liz, Dr. Hammond &
Mary Lou Pluemer**

Being familiar with the study's origins and objectives, I settled in with my fellow employees with ease. From 1972 until 1979 I searched for records on people who had been in the original survey. I traveled with Jane Laessig, Margaret Langdon, Gloria Cigalini, Haven and Ruth Kaslow among others to so many places: Boston, Baltimore, Harrisburg, Seattle and Minneapolis to name a few.

What a wonderful and dedicated group of individuals wholeheartedly tending to the task. We soon were all fast friends and visited each other's homes on weekends and while working in their home areas. While staying/working in the New York and New Jersey area, I met Detective Chuck Nolan who assumed the role of bodyguard and accompanied me through some rather unsavory places. What a wonderful, concerned and caring person.

If ever I got lonesome, I would contact one of my children who could get away for a couple days and come for a visit. They would help me with the paper work and when we'd finish, off we would go on an adventure touring the city, going to the theater, visiting museums or the battlefields of Gettysburg. We found some wonderful restaurants and ate "high off the hog". There was one particular establishment on the Baltimore waterfront I believe, that offered 13 different kinds of fresh vegetables.

My son, Patrick, ordered vegetables for his appetizer, vegetables for his entrée and, yes, vegetables for dessert. I have such fond memories of those many outings with each of my children that came to visit me, and I feel so very fortunate that we had those special times together.

DATE LINE

1972 Palestinian terrorists at the Munich, Germany Olympics, seize 10 Israeli athletes. 1 escape and 9 are killed

1972 CAT scans are introduced by British researcher, Godfrey Hounsfield, to look inside the human skull

1973 Syrian and Egyptian forces launch surprise attack against Israel. The Yom Kippur War prompted high inflation on oil around the world

1974 Bar Codes were developed

1974 The Watergate investigations lead to President Richard Nixon's resignation

1975 Video recorders come into the marketplace

1976 The supersonic transport, Concorde, begins regular transatlantic service

1978 The world's first ready-to-use personal computer goes on sale launching the computer revolution

1979 The Walkman stereo is introduced by Sony Corporation of Japan

1979 The price of oil doubles as the revolution in Iran spreads to other Middle East conflicts

1979 Mother Theresa is awarded the Nobel Peace Prize

1979 Elizabeth Roberts marries Francis Langeslag

1979 W.A.S.P.'s recognized as Veterans of the United States of America

Mother Theresa

RECOGNIZED AS VETERANS

During my years working for the Cancer Society I found myself in many different states, both mentally and physically. I tried to contact sister W.A.S.P.'s whenever I was in their 'neck-of-the-woods' from Washington to Massachusetts and places in between. It was so uplifting sharing accounts of recent events in our lives and memories of so long ago with someone who had been there. We had been so blessed. We had known the excitement of flying those magnificent war birds and, for many of us, the joys, rewards and hardships of raising a family.

We knew that the survival skills and self-confidence we had nurtured during our service years served us well during our life's missions. We had watched women ascend from the kitchen to the Congress, the Supreme Court, the President's Cabinet, cockpits of commercial airlines and to Commander of our space shuttle.

The sky was now the limit for what women could achieve and we had been there. We are proud of all that women have accomplished through the years and feel special ourselves in a reserved and old-fashioned sort of way for having been a part of it.

In 1976 national newspaper headlines stated that for the first time in history women were flying military aircraft down in Panama. We Women Airforce Service Pilots knew that announcement was not true. We had been slighted during our service, silent all these many years and now it was if we had never existed. Some of us W.A.S.P.'s decided to go to Washington and let them know they had 'misspoke'. Many Congressmen were very skeptical, and understandably so. Here was a bunch of 'old women' (actually we were only 60ish) with a lot of spunk, telling these young men and women, (who you can almost certainly be assured had never even heard of a W.A.S.P.), that as Women Airforce Service Pilots they had flown every type of military aircraft during the years 1943 and 1944. While they were checking and verifying our story the girls and I commenced a mailing campaign informing other W.A.S.P.'s of our activity and intentions. Many joined in the campaign and we showered Washington with notes and letters of our contribution to the war effort. The wheels of Congress do progress when prodded and on June 24, 1977, I received a letter from Ray Roberts, Chairman of the House Committee on Veteran Affairs, stating "...We have requested departmental reports from the Veterans Administration, the Department of Defense, and the Department of Labor on all pending WASP Bills..." While members of Congress were checking out our service records to determine our eligibility for Veteran status, Barry Goldwater was sponsoring just such a Bill. (Years later, after meeting Senator Goldwater at the Arizona Historical Foundation Lecture Series where he was speaking, I received a letter from him on February 9, 1996 saying, "What a wonderful surprise to meet you and receive your book...To be able to sponsor the WASP Bill and have it passed was one of the great moments of my Senate career...")

The G.I. Improvement Act of 1977 and Public Law 95-202, signed into law on November 23, 1977 authorized the Secretary of Defense to determine if our service in World Was II could be classified as active duty. After over a year of deliberation, on March 8, 1979, it was announced by Secretary of Defense, Harold Brown, that "... the service of the WASP had been determined to be active military service for the purpose of all laws administered by the Veteran Administration." After thirty-three years, we are finally recognized as veterans of the United States of America! I cannot express how this makes me feel and how very proud I am to be a member of both the American Legion Auxiliary and the American Legion.

**Liz in
Washington
D.C. 1976**

I still get 'misty' when I get to this part in my slide program. On May 21, 1979 the first Honorable Discharge from the Air Force was issued to a W.A.S.P. Recognition of our service was finally established after more than 34 years and, in May of 1984, we were awarded the World War II Victory Medal and the American Campaign Medal. My sister Mary deservedly received a flag for her coffin. We are so very, deeply grateful to all those who helped accomplish this.

LIFE GOES ON

Over these years, I returned to Faribault on at least a bi-monthly basis, and on one such trip during the winter, while trudging through the snow, my boot got stuck and I lost it in the depths. A man comes from nowhere, swoops me up and carries me into his house. Well I never! He went back and retrieved my boot, returned and asked what I was doing out on a night like this and where I was going. I was embarrassed, one of those red-faced moments, and told him that some friends and I were out for dinner and drinks and I had locked the keys in my car. Dear Harriet Steppan, who was in our group, lived five blocks up the street and, as I had done the deed, I was elected to go collect Harriet's' car. Without hesitating, he gave me the keys to his car and said to go pick up my friends, get each home safely and to forget about the car until morning. There was something magic about this chivalrous encounter. He was living in the house that my sisters' Cecelia and Mary shared during the 50's and 60's. Déjà vu. He had fixed it up quite nicely and when I returned his car, we had a spot of tea and, shy person that I am, told him all about my new job, family, connections and acquaintances in Faribault and such, and he shared part of his story with me and asked me to call the next time I was in Faribault. I found myself calling on every trip and making trips more frequently. He was a smooth dancer and we would do a turn or two around the dance floor at the Eagles, Legion or anywhere else we heard music. We even crashed a couple of weddings if there was a good dance band. After all, who was going to hassle a couple of 60 year olds.

In 1979, Francis convinced me to give up the road, marry him and settle into the comfortable life of the retired. In all honesty, I was a bit tired of living out of a suitcase and traveling all over the country. A different state every month was wearing me out.

I married Francis Langeslag on November 23, 1979 and that same year we visited Mesa, Arizona and rented a home until we found the nest we were looking for. We found it in Citrus Gardens Trailer Park and wintered there, seeing many friends from Faribault and meeting many wonderful people from all over during our seven-year 'sno-bird' residence. My Franny was diagnosed with Alzheimer's and died in March of 1988. The winter of 1986-'87 was our last Arizona winter in Mesa and may God bless Francis.

It was about this time that my brother George came to live in my upstairs apartment. We were like kids again. With our sister Cecelia and her husband, Dr. Art Bell, living close by, we always had a foursome. We played cards when we wanted, took outings to the Casino on occasion and they joined me in Arizona for at least part of the winter where we met with our sister Julia.

Elizabeth, Cecelia, George and Julia

Once again, life had smoothed out to an even keel. And then, wouldn't you know, during the Christmas season of 1990 at a singles party in our clubhouse I met Martin Strohfus, another man who really knew how to cut up the carpet. He had recently lost his wife and was just beginning to get out again. We had a lot in common besides dancing and there I again, we were married July 28, 1990. Life again had a regular ring to it playing cards, visiting friends and watching T.V., but we found ourselves going to more and more funerals. Every week we would visit the nursing homes, chat with the 'old people' and thank God for our health. It seemed we were losing our friends weekly either to the good earth or the nursing home. It was sad to see people without friends or family at this juncture in their life and I have to get down on my knees when I think how blessed I have been with my family, friends and health.

DATE LINE

1981 World's first reusable space shuttle,
     Columbia, is launched in April
1981 Egyptian president, Anwar Sadat,
     is assassinated by Islamic extremists
1982 The film, E.T., is released
1982 Compact discs (CDs) went on sale
1983 The camcorder is introduced
1984 British geneticist, Alex Jeffreys, suggests
     using DNA for identification
1985 The mobile telephone is introduced
1985 Mikhail Gorbachev comes to power in Russia promising
     perestroika (reconstruction) and glasnost (openness)
1986 Haley's Comet makes its regular 76-year visit to earth
1986 Chernobyl nuclear plant explosion in the Ukraine
1987 The fax machine comes into its own
1989 Convention on International Endangered Species
     imposes worldwide ban on trading in ivory
1989 Berlin Wall is torn down

Columbia piggyback

Haley's Comet

Hubble Space Telescope

1989 Tiananmen Square massacre of hundreds of pro-democracy protesters is committed by Chinese government

1990 Portable computers (laptops) come on the market

1990 World Population – 5.295 billion

1991 The Gulf War comes to an end with the liberation of Kuwait by an international coalition led by the U.S.

1991 Elizabeth flies F-16 with Mn. Air National Guard

1991 Bill permitting women pilots to serve in combat is approved by House panel

1992 Breakup of the USSR leads to President Gorbachev's resignation

1994 Elizabeth flies AT-6 for the <u>first time since 1944</u>

1995 The Hubble Space Telescope sends back high-quality pictures from outer space

Lovin' the T-6

PART II
Life Begins At 70

OUT OF THE CLOSET

I was sitting at home with Marty one day in 1991, when a young lady knocked at the door and inquired if I had been a W.A.S.P. during the Second World War? I told her that yes, I had been. She asked if I might have a few minutes to tell her about our organization. "You want to know about the W.A.S.P.'s? Are you sure? That was over 47 years ago." She explained that she was a teacher and was interested in educating her students about 'little known' accomplishments of women during WW II. She wanted to make young girls aware that such an organization of women pilots did exist during the war. Wow! This teacher had actually found out about our group, looked me up and had driven over 60 miles for a few minutes of my time. I was truly impressed, and a few minutes turned into about a six hour visit when she finally took her leave. Until then, she had read only one line in a history book that said, "There were 1074 women who received their Army Air Corps pilot wings during the war." That was it. After our interview, that one line became a more complete picture of the duties, lives and times of our W.A.S.P. squadrons.

My interviewer's name was Cheryl Young and she was curious about what we had done, where we were from, what we were doing now, how many of us were left, and, oh, just anything about this unique bunch of rare birds. Can you believe it? She was taking notes! At first, it was difficult putting those years in order and trying to recall some facts and events; not because I had forgotten or was suffering a so-called 'senior moment', but rather that I really had not thought about those years for such a long, long time. My brain was just too full of other stuff from over a lifetime. To get me on track, she asked if I had any memorabilia or pictures from those years. Of course, it's all in the back of my closet where it's been since about 1947. Long ago I told my children to pack it away with me in my coffin when I die because I was the only one to whom it meant anything. I started taking out my uniforms, scrapbooks, rosters, my Avenger Field Diploma, pilots' logbook, Honorable Discharge and so much other long ago forgotten about stuff. Each item sparked such vivid memories, in full living color to boot. It seemed unbelievable that this part of my life had happened so long ago and that it was _my_ life.

Cheryl developed a slide presentation for me and together we launched a speaking tour billed as 'Women in Aviation Presentations'. I absolutely could not believe the reception I received everywhere I went. The interest was evident by the questions asked. I spiffed up my uniform that still fit. I weigh about the same now as I did then but the weight is redistributed a bit. I went to clubs; American Legions, V.F.W.'s, Rotary and Elks but my favorite settings were the schools. All that wide-eye innocent potential was hanging on my every word. Fresh scrubbed faces, bright eyes and a manner

Liz and Brownie Troop

unspotted by the troubles of the day made them all truly precious. I would bring along models of the planes I had flown and the medals awarded me. They were fascinated and puzzled about the war and why they made girls fly airplanes. One little fella kept looking at me with an intensity I could not help but notice. When he knew he had my attention, he said in all seriousness, "Lady, for having such a old body, you sure got a young head." What can you say to that? Another day while showing the slides, I flashed a picture of our Fifinela, our Gremlin mascot with the wings. This third grader kept putting his face in front of the projector looking down into the lens. He would look down the lens, then check out the projected picture on the screen and repeat the process. Everyone noticed this sequence because his head would block out the picture. Finally, with a most puzzled look on his face, he raised his hand and asked, "Is she really in there?" I love them all, you just have to. So young, so thirsty for knowledge even if it stays with them for a short time. The seed is planted. I tell them they can do anything in the world they want, as long as it's not immoral or illegal. To follow their dream wherever it leads. The possibilities are legion.

I have spoken in just about every venue imaginable other than on a cruise or a space ship. I have been at airports, clubrooms, school auditoriums, hotel ballrooms, casinos, libraries, museums, city parks and cemeteries. I have been so fortunate to have been able to tell a story that I love to countless people who have had a real interest in listening and a genuine care for my well being. The doors opened for me since my 'debut' in 1991 have led to the most wonderful and exciting of adventures.

To present an overview of all these many outings, there are a number of organizations, associations, events, schools and settings that represent the core of what was revealed behind those many, many doors that made it possible for me not only to revel in reminiscing about those war years but to relive some of those memories and soar to never before dreamt of heights.

CONFEDERATE AIR FORCE
Southern Minnesota Wing
Ghost Squadron

The C.A.F. (Confederate Air Force) works to acquire, restore and maintain a growing collection of World War II vintage aircraft in flying condition. They also maintain an impressive fleet of WW II Vintage motor vehicles and display many other WW II uniforms and artifacts in their museums. The American Airpower Heritage Museum and Library, located in Midland Texas, is a great venue for students, teachers, historians and our public at large to learn so much more about this era with the added advantage of seeing and touring these war birds. As an educational and research resource, they preserve an impressive collection of World War II military aviation history.

Liz and Tuskegee Airman Harold Brown

The Southern Minnesota Wing of the C.A.F. headquarters at Flemming Field in St. Paul displays meticulously restored vintage aircraft including a **B-25 Mitchell** twin–engine bomber, **BT-13 Valiant** used as a basic trainer, **Harvard Mk IV**, also known as the **AT-6 Texan**, the advanced trainer, an **L5 Sentinel**, one of the Liaison and Reconnaissance Aircraft, a **PBY Catalina** – Amphibious Patrol Bomber and a PBY Civilian Fire Bomber, Tanker115, and the beautifully restored **P-51C Mustang**, an Advanced Tactical Fighter, one of only four of its kind still flying in the world! The Red-Tail, was the signature of the Tuskegee Airmen, an all black squadron who didn't loose one single bomber they escorted over Europe. You really should check out their story! Hats off to you guys.

We attended a C.A.F. Air Power Display at Holman Field in St. Paul during August of 1991. We met the most fascinating group of WW II veterans displaying their wares and sharing stories about their lives. Other than our W.A.S.P. reunions, I cannot remember when, if ever, I had enjoyed and participated in a weekend in which talking about flying and memories were the primary focus. The interest in caring for these beautiful planes was a most worthy project to become involved with and I have since attended every event possible.

Class 44-1 reunion in Faribault 1987

On September 13, 1991, I received a letter from Col. John Schuck of the C.A.F. honoring me with a commission in the C.A.F. and on my 80th birthday, November 15, 1999, I was presented with a Life Membership. I am truly blessed with so many wonderful friends and meet more at every event they sponsor, whether Air Display Show or HangerDances. Oh, to hear and dance to the Big Band sounds in a WW II hanger under the wing of a B-25 with a crowd of happy dancing people is something everyone should enjoy at least once in a lifetime, and it stirs such special memories for me.

80th Birthday with family

I am so lucky to have lived long enough to be able to share this next story with you. On August 2nd of 2001, the Gulf Coast Wing of the C.A.F. from Houston, Texas flew their B-17 Texas Raiders, to Owatonna, Minnesota to help advertise our C.A.F. sponsored upcoming Air Display Show the next weekend at Flemming Field in St. Paul. I was asked to be on hand to talk to the visitors and drum up some interest for the airshow. During the course of the day, the crew found out that I had co-piloted this plane so many years ago. I did raise a few eyebrows with that bit of information. We had such a fun, long day, even though the temperature was unseasonably hot. Well,

Liz and her B-17 "Texas Raider" crew

later that evening they called my son Patrick and asked if I might be interested in a media flight in the B-17 to St. Paul and back the following morning. Normally he would check any appointments with me, but he went ahead and said that even if I had an audience with the pope, I'd be on that plane. (He said it, so thank goodness I don't have to answer for it) At 9:30 the following morning we arrived at the Owatonna airport. I was so excited I was totally beside myself. As we're signing the manifest, someone called in and cancelled their seat. Can you believe that? As luck would have it, Patrick was standing right there when they were looking for the replacement. What a thrill! I was piloting a B-17 for the first time in 57 years with my son positioned as bombardier at take off. You know, it felt as if it were yesterday. The round trip, though it took most of the day with the media and all, went by in a flash. To have such wonderful friends to share such a day with and having my son along for the ride was truly a blessing. Telling this story in my slide show still gives that spine tingling sensation AND

And Still Flying...

MIST TO MY EYES. For your mission, for your maintaining our war birds, for your friendship and for your support I just love each and every one of you and may God bless you all.

MINNESOTA AIR GUARD MUSEUM

The M.A.G.M in St. Paul/Minneapolis houses the largest display of jet fighters and other aircraft from WW II, Korea, Viet Nam and the Gulf War. Among them are some of my 'old friends' the AT-6 and a P-51. One of the most sinister looking of all planes ever, the SR-71 Blackbird, stares at you as you enter the Museum parking area. I just have to shake my head whenever I see it and think of its story. This craft has to be re-fueled as soon as it is airborne because it uses and looses so much fuel on take-off! There are also a Boeing C-97 Stratofreighter, C-130, C-47 Skytraining Dakota (the Gooney Bird DC-3). An F-4C Phantom II, A-7 Corsair and a Huey Helicopter. Among their 6 simulators is a C-130, which I was lucky enough to have a go at. While attempting to fly beneath a series of three bridges over a river, I'm afraid I committed what is classified as a 'fatal error'.

I was so happy that 64 million dollar piece of training equipment was only a simulator! Never the less, I received my certificate. Inside the Museum are uniforms, flight gear, photo gallery and an assortment of Flight Manuals including one for the P-39 that I could certainly have used back in 1944.

The C.A.F. and Minnesota Air Guard hosted an 81st birthday party for me at Flemming Field in November of 2000 and my good friend Ray Peterson with the Air Guard presented me with an Honorary Membership in their Minnesota Air Guard Museum. You're all so good to me I often wonder why I'm so fortunate. I have received so much from so many wonderful people that I can't possibly mention you all, and for that I am truly sorry. But rest assured that each of you is in my prayers along with my heartfelt gratitude. However, I must mention John Bucigelupa who presented me with a picture of our Fifinella that he drew himself. I have it hanging on my wall next to a piece of the fuselage of an A-T 6 with my call numbers stamped on it made by my good friend and supporter Paul Scharffbillig. Paul and his friend Andy Burgess with his mother Bonnie have helped both myself and our friend W.A.S.P. Micky Axton with events and logistics over many years.

I was on the podium at an air-display show with Gen. Eugene Andriotti, Adjutant General of the Minnesota Air National Guard, enjoying all the activity when the General pointed towards an F-16 parked on the flight-line and asked, "You ever flown in a jet, Liz?" I told him the boys would never let me near a jet. "How would you like to fly in one?" "Would I, would I, why I'd be thrilled!" He said to go home and write a letter about why I wanted to fly a jet. On the way back to Faribault, I'm not certain whether I was going the flow of traffic or setting it. I was going over and over again the text of my letter. It had to be better than good and it had to be from the heart. I had to explain why I should fly a jet. I was up most of the night on this mission but when I re-read it in the morning, I was satisfied with the final version. I took the envelope directly to the Post Office not because I wanted to take the fewest chances of its getting lost or misplaced but to get the earliest possible postmark. Now it is in the hands of the General and the good Lord. Well, I waited, and I waited. After two weeks I was sure they had either forgotten about me or dismissed the idea of my flying. And then the phone rang. I just looked at it for a moment and said a quick prayer to all the saints in heaven so I wouldn't miss anyone and then I picked up the phone. It was the General. Oh, I just held my breath and then he asked when I would like to go flying? I answered, "Is right now too soon?" He had to get permission from the Pentagon and they asked if he thought 'this person' could handle a flight in an F-16 because not only was I a woman, but I was 71 years old!

General Eugene Andriotti, Liz and her F-16 pilot, Tim Cossalter

And you know what my good friend the General said? "I don't know anyone that could handle it better."

On August 28th of 1991, Cheryl and I made the trip to Duluth, MN where the 179th fighter wing is stationed and I was bubbling over with excitement. I could hardly contain the anticipation. It's good I got most of this wide-eyed emotional stuff under control during the 3-hour drive because when we arrived and finished pleasantries, joyous greetings and photo sessions with all the media, I was escorted to have my flight suit fitting by SMSgt Bruce Brostrom. I couldn't believe all the equipment I was carrying. There was the g-suit, helmet and a thirty-pound pack for my back. I had a rope in case I got stuck in a tree so I could lower myself down and a raft with a paddle to get me back to shore. I had a big knife and all kinds of ready to eat food. Getting introduced to all this gear was really very interesting. Then there was the familiarization with the controls in a simulator. All that electronics! Amazing. There was even a radar screen that could show you every plane in the area. My pilot, Lt. Col. Tim Cossalter explained that the yellow handle between my legs was the ejection lever. One of the reporters asked what I'd do if I was told to eject? I told him I wouldn't need a second invitation. And the joystick on that plane only moves a quarter of an inch. In my old war birds you could have both hands on the stick and really move it around. Another reporter asked Tim what he was going to do. Tim said he'd keep it straight and level and as gentle as possible. Hah! Now is the time for launching. I had giant butterflies as I climbed the ladder. I was secured and signaled thumbs-up and ready. Wow!

"THEY CAN HAVE THEIR '20,000 LEAGUES UNDER THE SEA'---GIVE ME 20,000 FT. UP IN THE AIR, JUST LIKE THAT (SNAP OF THE FINGER) ANYTIME."

Wow! What a rush and I really mean, what a rush. We flew formation with another F-16 for a while and then broke away. Tim asked what I'd like to do and I said "you said this baby could fly so show me." Wow! He knew maneuvers I had never even imagined. After enjoying the acrobatics of a lifetime Tim asked if I would like to take control. What do you think I said? He held his hands above his head and she was mine. Oh my, oh my. What a feeling. I said I was going to make a slow turn and phew, just like that the g-suit inflates as we flash into a dive. I was told that only a quarter of an inch movement would make the plane respond and they were not kidding. You can just think about making a turn in this jet and you've done it. Tim says, "Hey, take it easy back there 'cuz' I don't have the brown bag up here." I said, "That's O.K. Tim because I don't need mine." What a thrilling joyride. We were up for over two hours and then time for home. Such a shame. We buzzed the field twice before landing. There were still many reporters standing about who I'm sure were waiting to see an old lady getting hauled out with a derrick. I could have floated to the ground because I was still on cloud 9, and 10 and more. I was just overcome with the thrill of it all. I thought I had died and gone to heaven. I hadn't felt like that since, well you know.

I have given many presentations to and participated in Minnesota Air Guard displays and exhibits whenever I am able. It is always such a joy being with all these wonderful, caring and accommodating people. They are all so good to share their time and knowledge with the children and adults answering all the questions and ready to recruit for the Air Guard. Ray, Ron, John and their crew display a Phantom Aircraft mock at many air shows and parades. Everyone so enjoys the hands on and getting a picture taken being in the cockpit. (Being 82 eases my dismay somewhat not remembering so many names that I really should, but know that you are not forgotten) I could never express completely my indebtedness and gratitude for all the memories and happiness the staff, members and volunteers of the Minnesota Air National Guard have given me. Thank you all from my heart and may God smile upon each of you.

WINGS OF MERCY

I have presented my slide-program to many different groups in different parts of the country from Massachusetts to California and a few in between since 1991. I have always been well received and applauded, even if only out of politeness, and I am still somewhat amazed that people really do enjoy the history of the W.A.S.P. I have come in contact with a number of noble and notable organizations throughout the country, many of which I never knew existed. At the top of my list is The Wings Of Mercy. I was invited to be the guest speaker at their 1999 Banquet. This group, this wonderful association of pilots, doctors, nurses and other medical and mechanical support personnel, donate their planes, time, skills and energy to provide free air transportation for patients with limited income who need specialized medical treatment.

Liz & Glen Young

This is a volunteer group that flies these patients to treatment centers that are distant from their homes. Nearly 80% of the patients carried would not be able to have these specialized services without the generosity of the Wings of Mercy, who can only succeed through the graces of their members and the support from any who see this as a necessary and worthy organization. To learn more about the Wings of Mercy, contact Glen Young toll free at: (800) 98MERCY.

THE NINETY NINES

The Ninety Nines are an International Organization of Women Pilots promoting aviation and helping in community projects such as flying blood for the Red Cross and working with the American Cancer Society during their daffodil sale. I joined the 99's in 1945 and have been active on and off ever since. During the 1960's my friend and Charter Member of the Minnesota 99's, Rita Orr used to fly me to our meetings and on runs for the Cancer Society and Red Cross. She was my only link to flying and getting me to meetings. I really appreciated the flights and now I attend meetings and other functions, as I am able. The 99's has been a very special part of my life and even after being absent for a spell, it's always like old home week when we get together. I can never express how touched I am that this group has both inducted me into the Forest of Friendship and nominated me for the Minnesota Aviation Hall of Fame. Each was a great honor and humbling experience.

FOREST OF FRIENDSHIP

With Mn. 99's along the Walk of Names in the Forest

A credit that is so close to my heart is being honored at the International Forest of Friendship growing in Atchison, Kansas. The Forest is a living memorial to the World History of Aviation and Aerospace honoring those who have or still are contributing to all facets of aviation and aerospace with over 700 honorees. Atchison was the birthplace of Amelia Earhart, who, besides all else, was the first president of the Ninety-Nines, an international organization of women pilots. The City of Atchison and the 99's made a gift of the Forest to America on the occasion of Her 200th Birthday. I'm humbled being in the company of such notables as Amelia Earhart, Charles Lindberg, the Wright Brothers and General "Jimmie" Doolittle among so many others. It was the Minnesota chapter of 99's that nominated me for this plaque in 1994 and I am most appreciative.

I had hurt my back at that time and was laid up, so my Minnesota 99's accepted the award for me.

In 1995, friend and fellow 99, Bev Turk and I flew down to Atchison and I was so proud to be recognized by that group. To be present for the pageant when the new honorees are announced is almost a holy experience. Trees from each of our states and territories and thirty-five other countries from around the world are represented, with each state, territory and country flying its particular flag and the vista is breathtaking.

In 2000 our W.A.S.P. Class of 44-W inducted our dedicated, well deserving and great Class Recorder, Jeanette Jenkins, into the Forest. Wouldn't you know, she was unable to attend so I rode down with 99's Nancy Walsh, Bev Turk and Debra Nepple. Such great fun and so touching to accept the award for our friend and fearless leader Jeanette. 2001 brought Mike Vincent from Flagstaff, Arizona to drive Bev Turk, W.A.S.P. Micky Axton and me to Atchison for the yearly event and celebration. Mike is a great supporter of the W.A.S.P.'s and is such a fun and adventurous young man to be with. We saw so many of our friends and enjoyed the trip immensely.

Liz and Micki Axton at the Forest of Friendship by statue of Amelia Earhart

PRESENTATIONS

Since 1991 I have been asked to tell my story at all sorts of venues; from elementary schools to Rotary Clubs, from Legion Clubs to Ladies Groups, Air Shows to the State Fair of Minnesota, radio talk shows to library open houses and many, many others. I am always pleased to share my memories with anyone who cares to listen. I love them all, but I really do enjoy the elementary schools with the children so curious about this 'old lady'. They are so precious with a lifetime to look forward to and don't really understand the beauty of that. I would like to mention just a few of these engagements that stand out in my memory as notable.

Oshkosh Air Show

In August of 1992, I delivered my slide program to the Sea Plane Base Group at Oshkosh, Wisconsin. Bill McCarrel was an avid supporter and introduced us to Dennis Parks, Director of the Oshkosh museum who in turn invited me to speak at the Air Show Forum Tent 10 and Museum during the internationally attended Oshkosh Air Show. Peggy Baty, sponsor of the Women in Aviation organization, arranged for us to stay at the Jesuit Retreat House adjacent to the Sea Plane Base on Lake Winnebago that was such a beautiful setting. Our good friend and host Father Dick McCaslin was Director of the Retreat House.

My programs were well received and I met many wonderful pilots and friends with whom I keep in touch with to this day. I was aboard when Patty Wagstaff was featured at the museum. She has won many honors and was the U.S. National Aerobatic Champion.

I spoke at this air show in the years 1992-1995 and these years were such a wonderful experience. I was so fortunate to share them with my two sisters, Cecilia and Julia, and my sons Arthur and Michael and their families. Our stay at the Retreat House with other W.A.S.P.'s and friends was really the springboard and 'tone setting forum' for my on-going speaking tour.

Gathering of Eagles (November 3, 1995)

A most impressive WW II extravaganza was called "A Gathering of Eagles" orchestrated by Bryan Moon and Dr. Tom Wier, President of the Air Guard Museum. The speakers' were billed as a gathering of WW II aces. I felt somewhat out of place sitting on a panel with Battle of Britain squadron leader, David Glaser, R.A.F., Col. Hank Potter, B-25 pilot with Doolittles' Raiders, Col. Norman Appold who flew the low-level raid on Ploesti in1943, Lt. Col. Harold Brown of the renowned and highly respected P-51 Red-Tail pilots, known as the Tuskegee Airmen, Col. Robert Morgan pilot of the B-17, Memphis Belle and Lt. Col. Fred Olivi who co-piloted a B-17 during the bombing of Nagasaki. I was truly honored to be among these gallant men. What a fabulous event!

Eighth Air Force

Larry Bachman, President of the Minnesota Chapter of the Eighth Air Force, invited me to speak at their Christmas Program in 1999. It was held at the beautiful Mancini's Restaurant in downtown St. Paul. My sister Cecelia and son, Patrick, were along for the ride-and what a ride it was! I had given a program at my granddaughter's school in Madison, Wisconsin two days before and we launched from Madison on Sunday down Interstate 90 post-haste to arrive in St. Paul on time. I was most welcomed and have since had the pleasure and distinct honor of attending other meetings where we heard the stories of other of their members. I am most humbled at being party with these remarkable heroes. My stories seem so remote and almost inconsequential in comparison. The reality of war as they fought it and as I helped prepare for are worlds apart and I can never express my indebtedness for what they did way back then enabling me to do what I do today.

Association of Naval Aviators

I shared my program and stories with this great group in early 1996 and on May 30, 1996 they presented me with a life membership to their organization. I attend as many meetings as possible and especially enjoy the "Flight Jacket Night" when everyone wears their flight jackets and I am one of the judges (often with my sister Cecelia) to choose the best. What a difficult JOB! They are all the best and truly my heroes. Their experiences and successes throughout life are truly inspirational and a credit to all that is great in this great land of ours. Jerry Unruh, Bob Kruse, Dick Hill and all the members are such endearing people and such good friends.

Flight jacket night

I Can Fly

This was a celebration in Owatonna, Minnesota to promote flying and related fields that began in 1993. I had recently fallen off a runway on a cliff over-looking a lake used for hang-gliding takeoffs and injured my back, but was determined to be on hand. Karen Myers a pilot and a member of the 99's asked Cheryl Young and me to help organize and promote this event with personal appearances and newspaper and radio advertising. This event was held for three successful years until improvements began on the airport and access road making the airport inaccessible. "Buzz" Kaplan, another Minnesota Aviation Hall of Famer, was most instrumental in these efforts and realized a dream of his by opening the Heritage Halls Museum adjacent to the Owatonna Airport. This museum with its 'hands on' playroom for children of all ages (at 80, I enjoy this room quite as much as my grandchildren including the virtual soccer). Buzz has been the driving force in bringing this magnificent attraction to Southern Minnesota and we are all indebted to him for this magnificent asset. Heritage Halls also displays pictures of each of the Honorees in the Minnesota Aviation Hall of Fame. This complex is truly a major credit to your legacy, Buzz. Many thanks to you from all of us.

The Show must go on

Department of Veteran Affairs

In January of 1993 I received a letter from Kathleen Ellingson, the Federal Women's Program Manager with the Department of Veterans Affairs, telling me that she had enjoyed my presentation at the Women's Equality Day Seminar at Fort Snelling the previous fall and would like me to be a presenter during the Women's History Month Program at the V.A. Medical Center in Minneapolis. I happily accepted the invitation and since then have spoken at several of their functions in Minneapolis, St. Cloud and Sioux Falls, S.D.

I attend as many gatherings as I am able. I do have to mention my dear friends Bernie Melter who was the Commissioner, Department of Veterans Affairs and Paula Plum, Assistant Director who have both been most supportive of our women in the military and take such good care of me during my visits. The Minnesota Women in the Military also hold an Autumn and Spring meeting at the Medical Center that is quite an event. Besides attending as often as I can, I have given my program to a most understanding and appreciative crowd. Just a quick aside while mentioning the V.A. Medical Center. Since being recognized as a Veteran, I have had the good fortune of access to the Women's Clinic at the hospital. It is through the good graces, healing hands and dedicated care of people like Dr. Ensrud, Trish and the entire staff at the Women's Clinic that I am still flying with level wings,...if you get my meaning.

Northwest Airlines

As I mentioned during my recollections of our deactivation transition period in 1944, my day arrives with Northwest Airlines. In 1997, 53 years after I had submitted my resume` complete with 4-engine rating, instrument instructors certificate and sea-plane rating to the airlines with the highest of hopes of becoming one of their pilots only to be turned down, I was invited to be the guest speaker at their annual shareholders banquet. The entire corporation's executive officers as well as stockholders were in attendance.

During the afternoon activities before the evening gathering, I was invited to the simulator building. Mr. Terry Marsh, the Chief Exec. of the simulator school at North West asked

Liz, Sandy Anderson & Terry Marsh

if I would care for a ride in a 747 aircraft simulator. Well, try and keep me away. We board the craft and wow, look at all those instruments, dials, gauges and heaven knows what else. Terry takes off and does the usual check out maneuvers. He asks if I would like to give it a go, and am I happy. After a few casual turns, banks and changes of altitude, I went for the four-point roll. That plane shimmied, shook and grumbled, but came out of the roll beautifully. He then said it was about time to be getting back to attend the banquet and would I like to land. (I really think that he thought landing was beyond something I could pull off without making the 'fatal error'.)
I looked at all those instruments, remembered the size of this jet and was flustered for a moment. Then I remembered the instruments on 'my' old war-birds. Air speed, altimeter, and level-flight indicator. I calmly asked 'at what speed does this craft land?' Well, I just set the controls at that speed, entered the landing pattern and wouldn't you know, I greased the landing. If I wassurprised though elated, Terry was stunned.

He said to do that again, so we backed the plane out and I greased it again. After the third landing, Terry says to me, "I guess you really can fly these planes." I answered that I had told his company that over 50 years ago.

When I was introduced to give my presentation I opened with this statement. "I applied to NWA in 1944 to become one of your pilots. I was politely told that although my credentials were impressive, NWA did not hire women pilots but the front office could use the likes of me. As you know, I told them what they could do with their front office Understanding the reality of women's status at that time, and the fact that there was no one in attendance at this gathering that was in presence in 1944, (all either retired or flying with the wings of God) I forgave them for putting me off, gave my talk to a most receptive audience and have had a most wonderful relationship with them ever since. I must thank them all for their interest in our present day mission.

Liz does a slow-roll in 747 simulator and greases 3 landings

P-47 Pilots

It is a small world. In the Fall of 1999, we were having our 62nd high-school re-union here in Faribault. Outside the door to our hotel function room, I was chatting with an old classmate, when this gentleman comes along and inquires what the celebration is all about. We get to talking, and it turns out he is visiting relatives in the area and was a P-47 pilot during the war and also graduated in 1937. From one 1937 graduate to another, one story leads to the next, I mention my involvement with the W.A.S.P.'s and he introduces himself as Marvin Rosvold and joins our party. He got to know a number of people in our group and informs me that he is coordinating a re-union for his flying unit scheduled for the next September and would like to hold it right here in Faribault. I asked if there was anything I could do, and did he have a role for me! I arranged the lodging for 15 pilots and their wives at a local motel, reserved the auditorium at Heritage Halls Museum for me to present my slide show and made arrangements for a dinner-party at a local restaurant. Such a warm, wonderful group of people. They presented me with an honorary Admiralship in the Great Navy of Nebraska signed by the Governor himself. A truly unexpected honor and one of those 'out-of-the-blue' treasured moments.

Bemidji

We drove so far north that we began speaking French! My sister Cecelia graduated High School with a fellow named Larry Erie who has kept in touch over all these many years. He and his wife, Gladys, have become the developers and Directors of Camp Dellwater, a Christian summer camp located outside of Bemidji, MN. An inspirational setting for our youth with the woods, lake, wildlife and all God's beauty. While we visited there was a church group from Northfield, MN, a town about 12 miles from Faribault, enjoying their weeklong outing. Larry invited me to speak at his American Legion Club in Pinewood, MN. in 2000. What a warm, endearing group. I hesitate to tell the whole story for fear of being misunderstood. We had our lodgings at the campsite and stayed in Larry's house. A most comfortable north woods cabin. After freshening-up after our 6-hour journey, we ventured off to the Legion Club in the North Woods. The building had no in-door plumbing, the electrical connections were of down-home ingenuous extensions and the 'necessary' rooms were honest-to-god out-houses. Even with these limitations, they put on one of the best potluck suppers I can recall. I mention this only to emphasize the wholesomeness and well-intended interest of this particular group of folks and their total acceptance of someone like myself who visits. I was reminded of an era of help thy neighbor, life is good, take care of the affairs of the day and enjoy the setting of the sun. This 'hall' was located in the middle of the woods with no immediate town or houses evident. I was curious how many people would be in attendance, other than the Legion members. As the time of my talk neared, the room filled to standing room only. I still don't know where they all came from, but was so grateful for their support and interest in what we did so many years ago. They actually 'passed the hat' to help defray my expenses for the trip and out-did many other of my outings. I happily returned in 2001 to give my program to the Lion's Club at noon and the American Legion Club of Bemidji for an evening program. That visit had the added natural intrusion of tornadoes, lighting like you read about and thunder that still echoes in my ears. What a Night! We all gathered in the basement of the lodge for comfort and nervous conversation. Thank God the morning broke with no one the worse for wear other than lack of sleep. I have to say again...the lighting was awesome.

Family Outings

It is always so wonderful to visit my children whenever and wherever possible. I have been so fortunate to travel to different states where they are living and if asked, am happy to give my program to my grand-children's schools   I usually carry my slide

program and uniform for these occasions. I have spoken in
29 Palms, CA a number of times for both Kevin and Mary Carol's
daughter April and Julie's son Mathew. While Julie was living in
Massachusetts, I spoke at Mathew's school and was invited back
if ever in the neighborhood. While staying with them, I looked
through my W.A.S.P. roster and found Anne Lesnikowski living
on Martha's Vineyard. We had never met but after a chat on
the phone, she invited me out to Vineyard Haven for lunch and
a tour. My daughter Julie, her son Mathew and myself boarded
a ferry and sailed off to the island for a truly memorable outing
with Anne. She was such a gracious hostess and we shared so
many stories and memories. She and her architect husband
had purchased a water tower and built their home around it.
And what a magnificent home it was! Thank you so much Anne
for your hospitality and God willing we'll meet again. While Joe
Strohfus, my husband Marty's son, was in the Air Force, I visited
both Virginia and Florida where he was stationed and gave my
talk to their daughter Amy's classes. During this same period,
Andy Fiolka, son of Lana (Strohfus) and Randy Fiolka, had
drawn the pictures published in the book, "My Grandma's a Pilot".
We had such fun working on this project and I talked to his class
in Sioux Falls, SD with his brother Alex. It is always so heart
warming to see Marty's children and I'm lucky enough to live
enroute from Sioux Falls to the twin cities where Beverly and
Richard's daughters reside. They stop by on each trip for
a chat and we usually get a bite to eat.

**With my
daughter Juli
& son Michael**

My son Michael and his lovely wife, Kate, live in Madison,
Wisconsin, with their daughter Brigid. I have been invited
on occasion to speak at Brigid's school and I am always happy
to do so. These outings led to a speaking engagement for Kate's
employer for a Veterans Day gathering that I will address later.

Dubuque Central Alternative High School

Though I have been fortunate to speak at many wonderful
schools from kindergarten through middle and high schools
to universities, with great teachers and students throughout
the country, I have to stand up and take my hat off and salute
the students and teachers of a remarkable high school in
Dubuque, Iowa. The mission statement for Central Alternative
High School is to "Instill responsibility for learning by offering
quality alternatives which promote social,emotional and academic
development." The staff believes that, given the fundamental
levels of health, safety, and caring, all people want to learn
and that learning should provide not only context, but also
consequence, making intellectual learning and character
development of equal importance. Central has approximately
185 students including about 45 behaviorally disordered and

20 learning disabled students. The majority of the students are enrolled at Central based on the recommendation of the two other public high schools or through a referral from a special education team. In my opinion, the students and staff at Central are achieving their educational objectives.

My first contact with this school occurred at a Confederate Air Force Show held at Holman Field in St. Paul in 1999. A young man visited my booth and was genuinely interested and excited about the contribution of the W.A.S.P.'s. He introduced himself as John Adelmann, a teacher at Central Alternative. He told me about a research project on World War II his students were working on and asked me if I would like to be interviewed. We exchanged phone numbers and not much later Central student Lisa Becker, who asked me many questions, seeking information on the W.A.S.P.'s and their contribution to the war effort, contacted me. Then in April, 2000, I was invited to be a part of the students' public seminar they organized to honor local Dubuque veterans in their community.

This event was called "A Tribute to Victory," and it was held in Dubuque's beautiful Five Flags Civic Center. Along with myself, the students invited Tuskegee Airman Robert Martin (himself a native of Dubuque), and Brig. Gen. Paul Tibbets, commander of the famous B-29 "Enola Gay" to speak at the seminar. Nearly 1,400 citizens came out that evening in April to marvel at what

the students had accomplished. This was a three-day celebration, and we were treated like royalty. Another teacher and co-host, Tim Ebeling, kept the pace moving, not overly tiring, but a lot of fun. My escort, Lisa Becker, hovered around me administering to my every need. She was such delightful company for the entire visit. I hated to leave for all the attention I received.

During my stay I talked with many of the students who had contributed to the book they created called, "A Tribute to Victory: Dubuque in World War II." The local publishing company Kendall/Hunt Publishers published this research project for the students. It eventually went on to earn a state of Iowa and a national history award for excellence in local and community history! During a conversation, one student said to me, "We're the throw always." It almost brought tears to my eyes, knowing of their accomplishments and the obstacles these students had to overcome to achieve them.

Over the years, other Central students have created research books that cover different time periods of our nation's past. In combined American History and English classes, they published a book on the Tuskegee Airmen, called, "The Tuskegee Airmen – Victory at Home and Abroad".

They have contributed funds to help restore a rare P-51 Mustang to honor these brave Americans. Another research book was called "The Long Road To Civil War – America from 1820-1861" and yet another book honored local Dubuque veterans who fought in Viet Nam. These volumes are beautifully printed and are ripe with documented historical facts.

John has kept in touch over these years, and I always enjoy seeing him and his wife Judy at air-shows. In October 2001, John, Tim and another generation of students completed their research and fund-raising project in support of the CAF's Southern Minnesota Wing's Red Tail Project with yet another public seminar in Dubuque. The Red Tail P-51 flew in to town, and the weekend events organized by the students made it possible for local citizens to meet three Tuskegee Airmen and see for themselves that beautifully restored aircraft at their airport.

Thank you to John and Tim for all you have done. I am so proud of all the students at Central Alternative High School in Dubuque, Iowa and their achievements accomplished with such respect and professionalism.

Tom Kapsner with award winning WASP exhibit

MUSEUMS AND EXHIBITS

I am so old now that I'm in a number of Museums as an exhibit. It's nice to be around to answer questions the proprietors have about arranging the material, explaining the details and hanging the pictures. A few of these museums have closed for financial, insurance or other such reasons. One case involving interrupted operations of a museum is the Heritage Halls Museum of Owatonna, MN. This is such an attraction for everyone in the area as well as tourists from everywhere that it hopefully will only be temporarily closed. It boasts a wonderful auditorium for speakers and an inventory of aviation and other historical movies or programs that can be viewed upon request. The collection of airplanes, cars, snow-mobiles and other assorted antiques including Casey Jones' locomotive engine is such an historical boon for the area, that the closing has become a major loss of an attraction that really should be available for education and enjoyment. Buzz Kaplan, his associates and volunteers deserve highest kudos for the job they have done. Their 'hands on' learning center is interesting and fun for anyone 8 to 80 or even 82!

Our local Rice County Historical Society Museum displays artifacts that date back to 1853. There is a stroll down 'Main Street U.S.A.' with exhibits from 1880 to 1925, a collection of oil and watercolor paintings by Faribault artist Grace McKinstry, a display of Sellner Manufacturing furniture, lamps and lesser known rides other than their world famous "Tilt-A-Whirl" amusement park ride that is still one of my, and always has been one of my children's' favorite. I have given my program at the museum in the Holy Innocents Episcopal Church, built in 1869, and was exhibited as local pilot and W.A.S.P. in 1999 for about 4 months. It really gave me a thrill being recognized as a Rice County person of note being exhibited next to Bruce Smith, the only Minnesotan to be awarded the Heisman Trophy along with all their many other treasures. Yes, he was the son of the attorney, Lucius Smith, whom I've mentioned earlier. Jon Velishik, the Museum historian, was so gracious and accommodating during this period.

Another great loss to our area was the closing of the "Planes of Fame" museum at Flying Cloud airport in Eden Prairie, MN. They had a number of my old war-birds including a B-25 on display. Such wonderful times we had at their events. During one weekend affair, a Joe Jarzinen, who I didn't even know, told his friends that I was more than welcome to stay at his home adjacent to the airport because he would be gone for the weekend. Imagine that! We had the key, made ourselves at home for the nights and left a thank-you note to our unknown benefactor. I did meet Joe at an air show later that summer and got to thank him in person. What a wonderful gesture from a nice young man. Besides so many other features and planes, the museum set up a W.A.S.P. booth with history text, uniforms and other assorted W.A.S.P. memorabilia. I was pleased to give them what I could. I received an invitation to a Chinese dinner party at the hangar for one of their yearly banquets. I took that to mean to dress up as Chinese as possible and bring your chopsticks. Well, I decked out in my closest outfit to a kimono and set off to the banquet with my son Patrick. Was I ever surprised when most everyone had his or her flight jacket and overalls on to enjoy Chinese food catered by a rather famous Chinese restaurant. No one else thought about a Chinese dress-up affair. The food was fabulous, we had a fine time and visited the Casino on our way home where I raised a few more eyebrows. You have to have some fun.

I have set up a W.A.S.P. booth at various air shows and exhibitions, often with fellow W.A.S.P. and dear friend, MickyAxton, including the Mustang round up. This boasts an impressive collection of P-51 aircraft as well as vintage Ford Mustangs. They are all such beautiful machines and a reminder of two different eras.

Liz and Attorney General Janet Reno

From the web page of Wings of the North museum, they arose from the vacuum created when Planes of Fame Museum relocated to California. Since their beginnings in 1998, they have hosted a gathering of P-51 Mustang fighters, the Mustang Roundup in 1999 and the Aquatennial's AirExpo in 2000 and 2001.

Wings of the North is a non-profit education organization dedicated to preserving and presenting aviation history.

In honor of the accomplishments of the W.A.S.P. during WW II, the Blagg-Huey Library at Texas Women's University is now home to the W.A.S.P. Collection: an historical compilation of service records and memorabilia of the women's experience in the military during 1942-44. The W.A.S.P. collection is part of a larger Women's Collection that date from 1936 and includes more than 40,000 volumes, subscriptions to some 130 women's periodicals, and approximately 105 manuscript collections, providing the university with an important and substantial database for research. A goal of the library is to establish a $1 million endowment fund to enhance the dissemination of the history legacy of he W.A.S.P. for future generations, increase efforts to gather oral histories from their members, publish the W.A.S.P. Newsletter and to maintain W.A.S.P. rosters.

Liz in a Mohawk at Anoka airport

The American Wings Air Museum is dedicated to restoring and promoting the role of military aviation and the technological advances benefiting humanity. The museum has restored aircraft to air worthy condition including the Viet Nam era workhorse, the "Mohawk". The AWAM, located at the Anoka, MN County Airport, has let our MN chapter of 99's use their function rooms for meetings and have given us great support.

I've shown my slides there to enthusiastic crowds and enjoyed an evening dinner banquet for the Wings of Mercy Group under the wings of their museum planes. Over the years, Mike Langer, May God rest his good soul, and Kari Friel, who is now flying commercially, have been enthusiasts and gracious hosts at our many gatherings along with the many other volunteers and devotees of the museum and gift store. The AWAM has many pieces of "Mohawk" memorabilia that has been donated to the museum. They also sponsor an EAA national young eagles program that has a mission of providing meaningful flight experience to 1 million young people by the 100th Anniversary of the Wright Brothers first powered flight and the 50th Anniversary of the EAA in the year 2003. Any young people anywhere interested in flight should contact their local airport and inquire about the closest EAA chapter who have dedicated pilots ready to introduce the beauty of flight to interested youngsters.

I felt a special belonging to the ranks of American servicemen when I visited the Smithsonian Institution's National Air and Space Museum W.A.S.P. exhibit. The reality of who we were and what we had accomplished came to blazing light. Hearing and talking have certain social amenities, but seeing is believing. To have our uniform and other memorabilia exhibited in our nation's museum was an ennobling experience.

Partly because of my visit to the Smithsonian, I became a WIMSA field representative promoting The Women In Military Service for America Memorial in Washington D.C. This dedication ceremony took place on October 17,18, 19 in 1997 and was presided over by Vice President and Mrs. Gore. Northwest Airlines provided transportation and arranged for accommodations at Michael O'Rourke's home outside Washington for Cheryl Young and me. Michael and his wife were more than gracious, generous and concerned hosts in a lovely home during our stay. It felt as if we had been friends forever and right at home.

There was such an overwhelming display of respect and patriotism that I cannot possibly describe. An estimated 6,000 people witnessed the groundbreaking ceremonies in 1995, and one can only imagine the numbers present at the dedication. This was a more than impressive event, it captured the involvement of women in U.S. military history since 1776. The inspiration, sacrifice and dedication of these women come to life anew in the fountain and reflection pool, the Semicircle and the Ceremonial Gateway to our National Arlington Cemetery. Someone once said that behind every great man, is a great woman. Those resting in Arlington National Cemetery have given their greatness that we might carry on living in this great land, and on approach to that honored and hallowed ground we are reminded of the over 2 million women who have served our nation in every imaginable capacity for over 226 years.

If I may quote from a brochure from the Memorial, "Welcome to the Women In Military Service For America Memorial, a unique, living memorial honoring America's servicewomen-past, present and future" Situated on 4.2 acres of land at the ceremonial entrance to Arlington National Cemetery, the Women's Memorial is the nation's first major memorial honoring women who have served in our nation's armed forces during all eras, in all services and in "We Also Served" service organizations. The history of women serving in defense of our nation began more than 220 years ago with the women who served during the American Revolution and continues with those who serve today."

Liz at the Women's Memorial in Washington, D.C.

TESTIMONY AT HOUSE SUB-COMMITTEE

Jeff Olson, the Director of Veteran Affairs here in Minnesota, and his assistant, Paula Plum, have always kept me informed about matters of importance regarding Women Veterans.

On March 14, 2001 I was invited to give testimony before a Minnesota House of Representatives sub-committee with two Merchant Marines, in support of W.A.S.P. and Merchant Marine plaques to be placed at the Veteran's Memorial with the other Services along the walk of honor at the Veterans Headquarters Building in St. Paul. I really had no idea of the role and unbelievable danger our Merchant Marines encountered. Now there is a story that should be heard! I was featured in their Congressional Monthly Magazine and, yes, we did get our plaques!

The Women's Memorial Washington, D.C.

INDUCTION INTO HALL OF FAME

With all that we have mentioned to this point, all of the wonderful organizations, schools and groups I have had honor to come in contact with, all the many, many people I have come to meet and all the many places I have had good fortune of visiting I must now give humble thanks and prayers for having aided in my being inducted into the Minnesota Aviation Hall of Fame. This is the honor of honors being in company with my real life-long heroes who make up this elite fraternity. That the 99's would consider me worthy and that the committee would accept my nomination was a moment beyond my wildest thoughts or dreams. For all those who submitted letters of recommendation or voiced positive words in favor of my belonging to such a group, I am forever grateful and indebted. That my life should be considered to have had some impact on the lives and directions of others is most gratifying. I cherish the thought and yet feel so small when considering the battles fought by so many of these honorees. My role as aviatrix has been blessed by a reckoning of the times and being in position to share a story little known yet well respected. I am most proud of the accomplishments of all our 'girls', yet in comparison to the reality of warfare, our deeds were exactly what they were: support in a time of national need. We did what we could do best, and we did it well. The recognition or glory we never sought as W.A.S.P.'s somehow has come to a life of its own during these times.

Liz receives plaque from Noel Allard, President Minnesota Aviation Hall of Fame

My son Arthur was married the day before and all my children were present at this tremendous event along with other family members and friends that the reunion alone would have been outstanding. To all be together for my night of nights, was more than a person should ever hope for. God has truly smiled upon me once again and I have not even died and gone to heaven yet.

**Hall of Fame
21 April, 2001**

VETETRAN'S DAY

The pace we now register as contestants in this human race has quieted the tolling of the bells for those 'old vets' who have fought their last fight. At our local Central Park Memorial Day convocation, we used to toll the bell once for each veteran that had passed on during the past year from our county. Now, as if one represents all, the bell tolls once and for all. Even with this new style, on this most special of special days, I solemnly recall the fears, hopes, needs and deeds of those surrealistic years of a world war beyond our doing and beyond our knowing. The many sacrifices of a nation thrust out of a depression to preserve the very foundations of that nation. The rapid changes of an entire society to prove we were up to the task without question, without hesitation. We felt the loss of too many young men and of too much innocence and too many dreams. This was a time advancing a generation without question of what steps to take next. I do realize that to have been there is dramatically different than reading about those years in a context of morality and common decency, but there was no other possibility to assure the treasured place we are today. We do not apologize; we only applaud the efforts of so many in the defense of so many more to secure a future of freedom for the generations of a nation yet to come.

Though each Veterans Day throughout my entire life has been a day of thoughtful reflection, quiet prayer and inward determination that the sacrifices of our many veterans, from each war, must lead to a better future for us all. I do what I do as a reminder to some and a first-time introduction for others what the veteran is and what it was like during my years of service.

Again, being invited to the elementary schools on this day truly brings to light in my eyes, what this day of remembrance is all about – the children. There have been Veterans Days when I have spoken to as many as 4 different schools. For many of these students, I am the first contact with a WW II veteran they have ever had. I am aware of the importance of my mission here and so often feel I fall far short of bringing the significance and consequence of this period in our history to light. But as a seed is planted, a hope is born. These children know this is a special day in America, with a break from regular classroom studies to gather in the auditorium and listen to stories from 'ancient history'. We WW II veteran's telling our stories now can only hope the reality of those tumultuous war years suffered through in this land of ours, will remind all future generations that there was a past generation who gave their all that those who came after might have their all.

70

My daughter-in-law, Kate Roberts, arranged for me to give a presentation at the Forest Hills Cemetery in Madison, WI. in November 2000. She is a grief counselor for Gunderson Funeral Homes in Madison. This year Gunderson's sponsored a ceremonial service on Veteran's Day. Removed from the V-Day parades, the lunches at Legion Clubs and other social gatherings, this Ceremony took on an air of significance of its own. The reverence afforded at this cemetery, the gathering of like-minded people joined in common bond to give tribute to our veterans. The arena set up by this caring business brought a whole new dimension to this honored event. The tent they had set up was huge, and still there were people standing outside. The young and the old carried themselves as if at a funeral for a dearly departed one. Milo Flaten, a soldier at the D-Day invasion, and myself were the speakers and what a humbling experience this was. The appreciation afforded us, and the interest in our duties then and our doings now, was most uplifting. To send everyone off in higher spirits, there was a fly-over by three WW II era planes. This quiet setting among the markers, this moving moment, brought a tear to many an eye and a shiver up many a spine.

The most spectacular Veteran's Day event I have been involved with was called, "I Was There" held at the Paramount Theater in St. Cloud, MN on November 11, 1999. My good friends, the Voth's, invited me to be among their many speakers for the evening. I have known Dickie Voth, President, Granite City WAVES #142 and her mother, D. J. Voth, WAVES National State Director and member of the Granite City WAVES from Minnesota Women in the Military gatherings over the years. They are such a dear and dedicated duo. John, D. J.'s husband, has been most interested, supportive and patient with all our doings as Women Veterans.

Dickie and D. J. were on the planning committee for this particular event, and what an orchestration they designed. The evenings performance began at 7:00 P.M. and we did not sit for our 'after the event cast meal' until after midnight! There had to be more than 1000 in attendance and not one-person left early or even rustled in his seat before the finale. The very nature of the entire evening demanded a collective, captivated audience, showing not only respect for the speakers and their stories, but a more than genuine interest and concern for the near unbelievable personal accounts of active service under extreme and brutal circumstance being shared with us. St. Cloud Mayor, Larry Meyer, welcomed us all to his City for this Memorial and Bernie Melter, Commissioner, Department of Veterans Affairs, gave an overview of what Veteran's Day is all about.

The Presentation of Colors, Pledge of Allegiance and National Anthem set the tone for the evening, but not the magnitude. No one could have foreseen the stirring emotional, physical and vibrational impact this series of speakers would have on a full house of sincere attendees. The highs and lows, the tears and laughs, the heart-rendering churnings and the heart-felt appreciation for so much strife that had happened so long ago: from WW I through Viet Nam and the Persian Gulf. How many of us can really know...how many of us really care? The essence of the program started with a WW I synopsis complete with songs of the era, from "It's a Long Way to Tipperary" to "Yankee Doodle Boy". Even to me, this was as much a survey of history as an acceptance of chronicled fact. It reinforced in me the almost impossible task of bringing to life events that happened way back then. With the introduction of WW II Pearl Harbor survivor, Ralph Krafnick, the tenor shifted to an almost visible present day unfolding of horrific and unprecedented details of specific theaters and methods of warfare that not only silenced the audience, but also took away our very breath away.

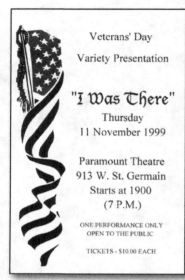

Veterans' Day
Variety Presentation

"I Was There"
Thursday
11 November 1999

Paramount Theatre
913 W. St. Germain
Starts at 1900
(7 P.M.)

ONE PERFORMANCE ONLY
OPEN TO THE PUBLIC

TICKETS - $10.00 EACH

Rosemary Krauel, of the Navy Nurse Corps, shared the bone-shattering truth of nursing the wounded and broken bodies of our servicemen and doing all one could to bring a moments relief from the pain, suffering and dying of injured soldiers. To be a medical care provider under the most extreme conditions demands a grit, determination and dedication beyond what is common or humanly possible. God has truly blessed us all with the presence of people like this in times like those.

And then Ken Porwoll was introduced. This man, this man among many men who survived and many more who did not, the brutality of the Death March of Bataan came to stage. He touched the very soul of us that makes us human, and the very heart of us that makes us American His memories of fallen brothers, his re-living an ordeal of extreme and inhuman measure, his tearful eyes and shaking hands, carried the hearts and souls of each of us to that god-forsaken, bestial territory from here to an eternity away. I cannot express the atmosphere in that auditorium as Mr. Porwoll delivered hisrecollections. The moment was infinite and the moment was immediately crushing. That such atrocities were even possible was beyond comprehension.

During his talk, it was almost as if there was a collective prayer being offered in unison for each and every person present during that evil action. And then silence. Total, revered and solemn silence. How do you follow a re-living of horror like that? Many a tear, but not a breath could be heard in that entire theater. were all exhausted and emotionally spent.

When my name was announced as the next presenter, it was like coming out of a deep, deep, nightmarish sleep. What could I say? My hands were clammy, my throat dry and my eyes weepy. What could I possibly say that would not dampen the significance of what we had just experienced by shifting the attention and yet retaining the mood of a most memorable and profound instant? I was beside myself. I was seated directly in front of my sister Cecelia and son Patrick. Cecelia took my hand and said, "be strong and carry on". It was a moment in the mist. I slowly walked up the stairs to the stage with tears in my eyes, facing an auditorium full of people stunned and saturated with visions of the most explicit humanly horrors, wondering what I could possibly say after what we had just witnessed.

I do believe that God intervenes on occasions of desperate need. I opened my mouth, and for the first time ever I said, "in 1991 I came out of the closet". After a moment of deafening hush, the relief of infectious, nervous laughter came over the audience. After all, it was Cheryl Young's asking if I had any memorabilia to refresh my recollections of where I had been and what I had done, that I first went to the back of my closet where I had stashed all my things from my W.A.S.P days. I can barely recall the remainder of my talk as I was still in the shadow of a very dark episode for so many of our men. To this day, that presentation was like living through an awake-state dream. I can only thank God for carrying me through that one.

Next on the agenda was a performance from the St. Cloud School of Dance exhilarating in 'Dances of the Era' including the Charleston and the Jitterbug. Such a wonderful and necessary relief! As I mentioned, the orchestration of this evening was very well thought through.

And then we had an animated and 'I was there' description of the "Battle of the Bulge" given by John "Hillbilly" Holt. So little we know about how much that had happened during this war truly amazes me. Every time I hear one of these stories, I wonder how much will be remembered after we who lived through it are all gone, but the graphic details must not be dismissed.

An entire not-so-new dimension of our involvement in this war and our continuing development as one nation under God came to the stage in the person of Ken Wofford, USAF, billed as an American Patriot. To be re-educated concerning our basic tenets of nationhood, to be reminded of our essential reasons for being and our very necessary next steps for a common bond in such times as these brought to vivid life what the higher purpose of Veteran's Day is ultimately about. To encourage understanding rather than resentment, to foster the requirement for personal growth and advancement rather than organized disenchantment and not to accept the way things are but rather translate them into a better place for us all through acceptance of how things ought not to be is the message I was blessed with hearing from Mr. Ken Wofford.

Again, there was relief from the intensity of this overwhelming convocation provided by the "Seams Like Swing Trio" (Andrews Sisters music). This interlude brought a smile to the face and put boogey in the feet giving way to a "Thanks For the Memories" tribute to Bob Hope. Chaplain Lt.Col. Father Harold Kost gave a blessing and prepared us for the second half of this unbelievable gathering.

Next up was a synopsis of the Korean War given by POW Kenny Hanson. The seemingly never-ending involvement in this crisis will certainly never come to full understanding or light by even the most dedicated of researchers. This was rather a lost era in a black and white world. So many people did not want to consider the reality of another war so close to the bloodied shirttails of so recent an atrocity as WW II.

Bernie Melter, USMC/Ret, presented an overview of the Viet Nam Conflict. This opens a door in our history that emphasizes all that is unacceptable in our modern day approach to the world and our treatment of returning veterans from unpopular wars. The aggressive, vocal and physical degradation of these veterans, the neglect of those who did not return and the status of so many of these service men today are almost embarrassing. We were given a statement about the Military Order of the Purple Heart during this war by Bill Woolies and Ron Kristopherson that makes me ashamed that I cannot do more. Not so much for recognition as needed assistance and acceptance was their testimony given. A feeling of what can we possibly do now overcame the audience and it was uniformly known that the answer was, very little.

Susie Warren changed the mood by telling us about "Operation Baby Lift". That there can be glimpses of hope and lives saved during such troubled times is always a Godsend. Thank you for your involvement and thank you from the children.

Cdr. David Wheat, USN/Ret, gave his account of being a Prisoner of War during this time and Oh how terribly awful! Army Nurse Corps, Lenea Wheeler, Col./Ret., gave her account of almost mission impossible proportions that again reminded us of where we had been and why we must keep up the 'good fight'. The songs "Blowin' in the Wind" and "Where Have All the Flowers Gone" were just the right touch during this part of the program. We were then given a Persian Gulf update with the American Flag being displayed as the North countrymen sang, "It's a Grand Old Flag". The traditional 21-gun salute was sounded as Al May and

Andrew Vavricka echoed "Taps". Young uniformed personnel enhanced the closing ceremony as Bernie Melter read a proclamation. Muriel Nissin led "God Bless America" from the Granite City WAVES as the Colors were retired. What more can I say about an event beyond expectation, an evening beyond belief. How grateful I am to have been there and should you want to enhance any Veteran's Day gathering for your Club, School or even family and friends, I do believe the video of this most remarkable symposium is available through the Granite City WAVES in St. Cloud MN.

THE PARADE

The only bad thing about being in a parade is that you don't get to see the parade. And I have loved a parade my entire life, whatever the occasion and however grand. Whether our local pet parade down 4th Street with all the dressed-up children, pets, bicycles, tricycles-cycles and wagons or the Rose Bowl Parade where I've been perched on the viewing stage. I've been so lucky to have been in more than a few parades over the years representing not only W.A.S.P.'s, but also Women in the Military, girl scouts, American Legion Auxiliary and even served as Grand Marshal for our Faribault Heritage Days Parade. I have ridden in everything from the limousine to a jeep, a beautiful convertible and on floats. I've been in the cockpit of an F-4 Falcon with my sister Cecelia, who wasn't overly crazy about the idea, and I have even walked the distance when able.

Speaking of Women in the Military, I have to say how proud I am of the heights our young women have soared to today. I have met so many dedicated young women -and men- at various R.O.T.C. and National Guard Unit events, my favorite being the Dining In. The pageantry at these events with all the uniforms, traditions and demonstrations brings a tingle to my spine. These cadets bring to life the reality of patriotism, show a genuine interest in history, are career oriented and carry themselves with such politeness and style that I can only be reinforced with highest hopes for tomorrow and highly impressed with them today. Just beautiful...all of them...just beautiful.

Liz and her sister Cecelia

**Main street
Faribault
1945**

And I have met Col. Eileen Collins who was the first female commander of our space shuttle. She serves as such a wonderful role model and hero for so many. As I said about an airplane not caring if the pilot is a male or female; all 'she' cares about is whether or not the pilot can handle her.

AIR SHOWS

**ELizabeth and
Col. Eileen Collins**

I love a parade but I am transported by an air-show. To know that almost frenzied, excited anticipation from the first plume of exhaust as one of these war-birds begins her ignition. The sputter, cough and stutter until she fires. Oh, that wonderful sound of the smooth roar of those planes as she catches. And in the air as they fly-by. To first see it, then begin to hear the roar of the engine until it explodes into the most beautiful thunder as she flashes by. I can hold that moment forever in my mind and rejoice whenever I think of it. That fly-by instant has been great therapy for me over the years remembering that I was there. To be able to judge, with some accuracy, the altitude of these 'birds' as they soar in formation or perform their aerial acrobatics. To recall the thrill of the spin and the circling horizon throughout a roll is such soothing elixir for these old bones. These are the best of memories for a 'more senior' pilot. I get tingles up my spine, a shortness of breath and a sense of accomplishment and pride knowing that I have done that and been there when called upon, and I am always hoping to be called upon again soon!

Holman Field in St. Paul used to host the C.A.F. air shows in the fall of the year and what great turnouts of enthusiasts we had. One year the temperature soared to most uncomfortable levels but even that did not keep the people away. Since about the year 1999, the air show has changed venue to Flemming Field, headquarters of the Southern Minnesota Wing of the C.A.F. in a WW II Quonset hanger. There is a museum, gift store and hanger space for a number of their planes. They hold hanger dances two times a year, and I have to tell you, if you haven't danced to the Big Band Sound provided by the Roseville Big Band, why you just are missing one of the most enjoyable, nostalgic evenings of dance, food, and upbeat company ever imagined in these modern times. Dancing under the wing of a PBY or the B-25 in the moonlight, will transport even the young of heart and stature, back to an era that earned each moment of joy it found. I am so happy to see so many young people taking an active interest in our swing style of dance and our style of dress. On these evenings, the hanger is filled to standing and dancing room only. Way to go kids and thank you C.A.F.!

If you care a whit about aviation and have not witnessed a performance of either the Blue Angels or the Thunderbirds, well you have missed the boat. The best of the best engaging in the most unbelievable formation, stunt and close quarter flying that borders on the limits of imagination and the physically possible. As important as a crowd-pleasing phenomenon, to say the least, these squadrons demonstrate the exactitude and precision of our military in action. Give yourself the gift of a lifetime and get out to an air show and experience one of these awesome units.

A Hanger Dance

Rather a personal side note on witnessing a Blue Angels show in Duluth. My good friend and supporter, Mr. Dick Williams, escorted Micky Axton and myself to an air show at the Duluth Air Port in support of the new Duluth Chapter of the C.A.F. This was the launch pad of my F-16 flight in 1991 and I have many treasured friends still involved there. On Sunday, for the Blue Angel air show, I was invited to view the spectacle from the control tower. WOW!!! These planes flew by so close I could have reached out the window and washed their windshields. The vibration in the tower was fantastic. The sound in the tower was deafening in a very satisfying manner. The view from the tower transported me right into the cockpit where I had once sat. I can never thank my very dear friend Ray Koslowski for inviting me to the tower and all that he has done for me over these years since my F-16 flight.

An air show that stands out was held in Mankato, MN. where the Thunderbirds were to perform. There was quite a low ceiling so most of the high level acrobatics were cancelled. But the show did go on. I had set up a W.A.S.P. booth in one of the hangers and was waiting for the announcer to introduce the Thunderbirds. Then, over the loud speaker I heard, "The Thunderbirds are now taking off from Minneapolis Airport about 70 miles away." Well, I barely got out to the field when whoosh there they go! Just minutes had lapsed since their taking off in Minneapolis. Now that was really something. And on a Memorial Day in Missouri for a WW II pilot recognition celebration I again was totally uplifted by the aerial extravaganza exhibited by our Air Force elite precision team, the Thunderbirds. They are always a joy, always a treat and always a head-shaker.

Liz and Dick Williams

One annual event I always look forward to is our Faribault Area Airport hosting the Balloon Rally. This is a weekend gathering beginning on Friday morning when I am usually asked to spend at the airport and talk to the 6th grade classes of Faribault that make a field day of it. I always enjoy being around the children and they are so keen and interested in all phases of aviation. Being at the airport, hanging out around the planes and balloons, hobnobbing with pilots and support personnel

First balloon ride certificate

and sitting in the cockpit of the Minnesota Air National Guard F-4, brings to life the beauty of flight and very attainable goals of becoming involved for all. The weekend includes an on-going air show, many remote controlled aircraft of every size, shape and form, a demonstration of ultra-light aircraft and, of course the beautiful balloons. Their Nightglow show is a most inspiring and glorious sight. I try to exhibit a W.A.S.P. booth for the weekend whenever schedules permit, and in 2000 the crew of the Phoenix Balloon were looking at my memorabilia and one of them asked if I had ever been up in a balloon. Wouldn't you know another door was opened for me to enjoy what Imost enjoy: Flying. I jumped at the chance and oh, what a wonderful flight in a hot air balloon I had.

SENTIMENTAL JOURNEY

In the bigger picture, my 15 seconds of fame may have been set in motion by my first solo in a 65 hp Piper Cub or maybe my encounter over the telephone with Cheryl Young who brought me out of the closet, so to speak. My heartfelt gratitude, respect and wondrous amazement at the feats and defeats suffered by all our boys in each theater of combat during WW II is only enhanced each time I hear one of their stories.

To be able to share my story from this same period with so many who have come to listen, I am humbled to the point of tears when knowing the awful sacrifices and inhuman horrors these boys endured. Having heard stories from the Bataan Death March, to the D-Day invasion. From bombing flights over Germany to ground fighting in Italy I am brought to the memory of the ultimate investment made by so many that has catapulted our nation to the Greatest Nation on God's earth. We are in position now to give aid and other assistance to so many countries of greater need because of what they have done.

The beautiful B-17 "Sentimental Journey"

My sentimental journey has made me so aware of all that was accomplished by our boys in combat and our 'Rosie the riveters', the medical corps and the farmers at home supplying the rations that maintained strength and stamina, the children who did, and those that did not complain about the rationing of certain goods and foods. Every person in this great nation of ours that lived through and supported this war effort, in whatever manner, holds the banner of victory that became ours because of this dedication.

Our thoughts and prayers go out to our service men in harms way: from the bomber crews and fighter pilots, to the infantry, artillery commands and ground support personnel. The little known accounts of our Merchant Marines and the Service Squadrons, the media groups and the Red Cross Units.

Every one who lived through these years and memories of those who died during these years have dedicated such devoted service to honor and preserve this land at war that we call America must never be forgotten. What words can truly express the demands placed upon our young men, the need for certain actions, the justification for such awful destruction as was witnessed during these years of World War.

MY GREAT SUPPORT CREW

As I fondly recall all that has happened in my life over these past 10 years, I am recharged by the input and energy of so many people that I cannot possibly mention them all. Above and beyond are my two dear sisters, Cecelia and Julie who have been patient to a fault with so many of my engagements, adventures and shenanigans. They have accompanied me to events and air shows whenever possible, encouraged me when needed, nursed me when I was ill and set me straight when they saw fit. We get a special pleasure when being referred to as "there go the Wall girls" or "if you see one red-head, count on seeing at least one more".

**The Wall Girls
Liz, Julia & Cecelia**

I must note just a few of those people who have opened doors for me, fed me and transported me to the next stops. Dick Williams of the C.A.F. has accompanied me on more than a few occasions and has invited me and mine to a gala event at his lovely home. Again, Ray Peterson, has given special attention and care to me over these years and been responsible for some notable outings including the flight in the C-130 simulator at Fort Snelling. He is also always looked for at our Balloon Rally here in Faribault. There are so many of you that I cannot mention but you must know you are all in my thoughts and prayers. But, Tony you must come to light. Photographer Tony Evans, my friend, has done more for me than I can ever express. His interest in all veteran stories, his dedication and professionalism at his art and his caring for those who care is overwhelming. He presented me with the most awesome Birthday Card on the occasion of my 80th that I can hardly explain. It was a collage of my life on a card that was 40"x32" in dimension. I don't have a wall big enough to give it justice. For all you have done Tony, thank you from the bottom of my heart.

**Tony and Liz's
grand-daughter
Kathryn**

SPAM WW II MEMORIAL DEDICATION

Sunday, June16, 2002 proved again to be a banner day. The Hormel plant in Austin, MN opened its Spam Museum honoring employees who had served in WW II. 1750 had enlisted and 67 of them had given their lives. There are 300 still living and many of them were present at this prime event. A large American flag served as the stage backdrop as Phillip Burnell directed the choral group in Patriotic songs. And I was privileged to be the Mistress of Ceremonies. The program opened with a fly-over by F-16's from Duluth -and I really could say that they were my friends. After chatting a bit as I do, I introduced Joel Johnson, CEO of Hormel, who in turn introduced our key-note speaker Tom Brokow. What a thrill being on stage with Mr. Brokow, news anchor and author of "The Greatest Generation". (I had my copy autographed). Tom opened his speech recognizing the the W.A.S.P.'s by saying,

> "...its hard to overstate the importance of those women who flew those airplanes and made it possible for us to get more men in the combat cockpits. And before the war was over those women were sent home without recognition for what they had done and without veterans benefits. And it was many years later that they finally did get the appropriate recognition and the veterans benefits. But they didn't whine and they didn't whimper and so they were emblematic of that great generation."

Mr. Tom Brokow in his turn introduced Mike Farrell, a FDNY Fire Marshall who was **there** and personally lost 20 close friends, represented his brothers in the Department and New York City as a whole like a gentle giant. His message was warm, encouraging and demanded a level of hope that is so needed. He went on to thank all America for their generous donations

**Mike Farrell, Tom Brokow,
Liz and Joel Johnson,
Hormel C.E.O.**

and prayers that helped bring his city back to some degree of normalcy. God bless you and yours Mike.

My sister Cecelia and sons Arthur and Patrick were with me for the day and were invited to a beautiful buffet brunch with the cast and crew of this fabulous affair. I even received a curious Spam can candle as a memento of the event.

THE IMMORTAL CHAPLAINS

As this story comes more to light, it immediately assumes a place of supreme honor that is representive of those holy, unselfish acts of heroism offered as a tribute to life and death. 'No greater love can man have than to lay down his life for his brother'.

The deeds of four U.S. Army Chaplains - Lt. George Fox (Methodist), Lt. Alexander Goode (Jewish), Lt. Clark Poling (Dutch Reformed), Lt. John Washington (Catholic) and the 672 brave men who perished with them inspire this Prize for Humanity.

In the darkness of February 3, 1943, the U.S. Army Troopship **Dorchester**, in convoy with three Coast Guard cutters and two freighters, was torpedoed about 100 miles off Greenland and sank approximately 18 minutes later. In that brief time, the four Chaplains calmed the men, distributed life jackets and helped some 230 safely depart the ship. When the life jackets ran out, witnesses observed the Chaplains remove their own, and without concern for race or religion, place them on waiting men. The Chaplains then gathered the remaining men on deck to pray and sing. As the ship plunged into the icy sea, the four Chaplains were seen standing, arms linked, in common prayer.

Their lives and their legacy are immortal and challenge us: "If they can die together, can't we live together?" This story is taken from the Program of "The 2003 Immortal Chaplains Prize for Humanity Presentation." This was for the many Service Volunteers of World War II and the Villagers of the Region Le Chambon-Sur-Lignon, France who defied the Nazi occupation orders by sheltering as many as 5,000 refugees (mostly Jewish) from deportation and extermination during the period 1940-45.

We were welcomed by Dean Garvin Davenport from host Hamline University in St. Paul MN. David Fox, nephew of Chaplain Lt. George Fox and Executive Director of The Immortal Chaplains Foundation gave a moving and inspiring closing that deserves close reflection by all present. The Presenter of Honors was U.S. Army Chaplain and Minnesota Senator Dean Johnson.

Representing all Women Service Volunteers of WW II, I received this award. Learning the scope of this honor leaves me without breath. Other recipients this year were Henry C. Scholberg for the Non-combatant Service Volunteers of WW II and Tom Oye representing the Combat Vounteers of WW II. The agent for the villagers of Le Chambon-Sur-Lignon was the mayor of that city, Francis Valla.

The message on the plaque itself was written by Secretary of State, Colin Powell. "...I hope you will take the time to savor the significance of this award. It is fitting and proper to reflect on the special patriotism that helps make certain the liberties and dignity of our beloved Nation. You are heroes and I wish for you a wonderful event filled with camaraderie and good fellowship..."

Past Recipients of The Prize for Humanity are Charles W. David an African American Coast Guardsman who gave his life in 1943 to rescue others from the sinking troopship *Dorchester*, Pastor Martin Niemoeller a German Lutheran minister who defied Hitler face to face for persecution of Jews and others, Father Michael Judge, OFM the Chaplain to the NYC Fire Department who refused to leave praying over a dying fireman at the World Trade Center, Sept. 11, 2001 and Archbishop Desmond Tutu among many others.

Humbled, grateful and breathless are not profound enough expressions of appreciation.

Liz accepting the award in recognition of all Service Volunteers of W.W. II

MIKES EARLY LETTER

10/2/74
Boston, MA

For my Mother,

It is only time and it is only distance that separates us. (Family love is not bounded by mere time or distance; it would take a universe to circle it.) Yet, your wings, so long folded, are loosed. You stayed long enough to see us grow and helped to show us how far our own wings would go. But now we've flown, and you go to view the world from different heights. Time and distance are little things to those with vision. They seem more awesome though with each passing month, and I think of you with care and wonder as to how you are, and where.

You know, now as I recall my more youthful days (it's not as if I've grown old, yet I'm older now) I can remember the love you gave us, though I didn't have a word for it then. There was something else, likewise until now unnamed; a certain spirit, a light in your eyes that shined at certain times. I've termed it a little bird, and I know she had her own special little nest in your heart.

I can remember the times when I saw that bird, that little bird of strength and spirit, that youthful bird of flight for freedom's sake. She would peek her head out from behind your eyes that she might view the sky on a pleasant day in our backyard. She would then, with her practiced eye, measure the distance from where you stood to the sky. She would check the direction of the wind using a drying bed sheet hanging on the line as a windsock. Or sometimes she would simply want to bask her face in the warm sun, and your eyes, dear mother, would smile at your private thoughts as if you soared unfettered by the ground, surrounded by gentle wisps of cloud. But always then, a shadow moved across your eyes and they would frown while the little bird looked down to view the delicate golden chain wrapped gently, but firmly about her wings. She would then retreat to that treasured loft in your heart with a sigh; you would shrug your shoulders just a little bit and go back to hanging clothes to dry; but then, you'd smile again, and I loved you for that.

This is just a note saying I love you still, and if the little bird needs shelter from some stormy night - she'll find it here. Or maybe sometime we'll meet in mid-flight and view the world from there.

Love always,
Your son, Michael

APPENDIX

LIFE SKETCH

BORN: November 15, 1919.

Graduated Immaculate Conception Elementary School in 1933.
Graduated Faribault Senior High School in 1937.

1937-1941	Worked at the Rice County Court House.
1942	Began Flying.
1942	Member Civil Air Patrol during WW II.
1943-1944	W.A.S.P.
Dec. 20, 1944	W.A.S.P. De-activated.
1945-1946	Aircraft Communications. (No Flying!).
1947-1948	Worked for law office of Lucius Smith.
Dec. 27, 1947	Married Arthur Roberts.
1949-1953	Had five children.
1959-1972	Continued to work for Lucius Smith part-time and returned to work at the County Court House in various offices finishing my last few years as assistant to the County Assessor.
1949-1972	Mother, Wife, Brownie Mother, Den Mother, PTA activist, Life Enthusiast!
Jan. 11,1969	Receives Honorary Scroll Award from Jaycees for Community Service.
Oct. 13, 1969	Husband, Arthur Roberts passes on.
1959-1972	Volunteer for the American Cancer Society.
1971-1972	Ran for Registrar of Deeds for Rice County. (Lost by 1 or so votes.)
1975-1977	Lobbies for Veterans Recognition for W.A.S.P.'s. Women Air force Service Pilots receive Veteran status with the G.I. Improvement Act of 1977.
1972-1979	Employed as Statistical Researcher for American Cancer Society out of N.Y.
Nov.23,1979	Marries Francis Langslag. Retires Cancer Society.
1984-1985	Winters in Arizona with Francis. Renews some flying acquaintances.
Dec. 3, 1988	Francis dies after long struggle with Alzheimer's.
June 6, 1990	Marries Marty Strohfus.
1991	Begins presenting her story and slide show to schools, organizations, universities, air shows and other groups.
1991	Flies F-16 out of Duluth with Minnesota Air National Guard at age 72!
1992-1997	Gives presentation at Oshkosh Air Show.

June 18, 1994	Honored in Memory Lane at the International Forest Of Friendship being nominated by Mn. 99 organization.
Sept. 2000	Voted into the Minnesota Aviation Hall of Fame.
April 21, 2000	Inducted into the Minnesota Aviation Hall of Fame.
Aug. 3, 2001	Flies B-17 from Owatonna, Minnesota to St. Paul, Minnesota at age 82!
June , 2002	Mistress of Ceremonies at the opening of the Veterans Museum at the Spam Museum in Austin, MN. Introduced Tom Brokow and Mike Farrel, a New York fireman who was there that awful September day.

ORGANIZATIONS

Military & Aviation

- Faribault Sky Club since 1942

- Faribault Area Pilots Association since 1942

- Women Air force Service Pilots
     (received WASP wings, Feb. 12, 1944)

- The Ninety-Nines, Inc. Minnesota Chapter since 1945

- Women Veterans Organization

- Women Military Aviators, Inc. (WMA)

- Women In Aviation (WIA)

- Association of Naval Aviators (ANA)

- Women Veterans Memorial in Washington D.C.
     (Field Representative)

- The Confederate Air Force

- Minnesota Wing 8th Air Force

- ADMIRAL: The Great Navy of the State of Nebraska

- American Legion

- American Legion Auxiliary
     President 1968-1970
     3rd District President 1972

Inducted into Minnesota Aviation Hall of Fame in 2000

Church Groups

* Member Immaculate Conception Church
* Knights of Columbus Auxiliary
* Daughters of Isabella
* Rosary Society of Immaculate Conception Church

Civic & Community

* Hospital Auxiliary
* River Bend Nature Center
* Rice County Historical Society

WOMEN AIRFORCE SERVICE PILOT STATISTICS

* 23 Women Pilots were accepted by the Army Air Force without formal Army Air Force flight school training but had 200 hours flight time known as the WAFS, (Women's Auxiliary Ferrying Squadron).
* 25,000 Women Pilots applied to the Army Air Force for flight training.
* 1,879 Women Pilots were accepted by the Army Air Force for the flight-training program.
* 1,074 Women Pilots graduated from the Army Air Force training detachment flight school at Sweetwater, Texas.

These Women Pilots were known as the 319th Army Air Force Training Detachment from October of 1942 until July of 1943, the 318th Army Air Force Training Detachment from July of 1943 to October 1944. In November and December of 1944 they became the 25630 Army Air Force Base Unit.

* 916 Women Pilots were assigned to active duty stations at the time of deactivation of the W.A.S.P. Program.
* 38 Women Pilots were killed during their tour of duty in the W.A.S.P. Program.

FLIGHT OPERATION STATISTICS
OF WOMEN PILOTS WITH THE ARMY AIR FORCE

- 77 types of aircraft ferried
- 12,650 ferrying operations
- 60,000,000 miles of operational flights
- 9,224,000 miles flown in ferrying operations
- 3,000 aircraft – 2/3 of all pursuit aircraft were ferried
  by 35 women at one ATC Base in less than one year
- All P-47 Thunderbolts ferried from Republic factory in the last
  half of 1944 were flown by W.A.S.P.'s.

TYPES OF FLYING DUTIES
ASSIGNED TO WOMEN PILOTS

- Ferrying
- Check pilot
- Demonstration
- Administrative
- Engineering test
- Radio control flights
- Simulated strafing missions
- Towing targets for anti-aircraft
- Towing targets for aerial gunnery
- Tracking and searchlight missions
- Smoke and chemical laying missions
- Flight Instructor – Basic and Instrument

PRESENTATIONS GIVEN BY ELIZABETH WALL
STROHFUS, W.A.S.P. FOR THE YEAR 2001

DATE   **ORGANIZATION OR SCHOOL**

Jan. 13   American Legion and Auxiliary Banquet Speaker
            in Hemet, Ca.

Feb. 10   At the Book Store in Hemet, Ca., autographed
            "Wingtip To Wingtip", a collection of stories about
            WASP'S, with author Margarite Roberts.

March 3	Gave program in the Pavilion for Veterans at the Ramada Express Hotel and Casino in Laughlin, Nevada.
March 14	Gave testimony before a Minnesota House of Representatives sub-committee with two Merchant Marines, in support of WASP and Merchant Marine plaques to be placed at the Veteran's Memorial with the other Services along the walk at the Veterans Headquarters Building in St. Paul. Was featured in their Monthly Magazine and, yes, we did get our plaques!
March 15	Gave my program to the Officers Wives Club in the Officers Club at Fort Snelling, St. Paul. Was enthusiastically received.
March 21	Presentation at the Sandberg School in Anoka, MN. to forth and fifth graders. Polite, well-disciplined children and they say the Pledge of Allegiance. Pleasure to see.
March 23	Gave a program for Home Schooled children and their parents at a Lutheran Church in New Prague, MN. Great group with some really good questions.
April 5	Gave presentation at a D.A.R. luncheon at the Fort Snelling Officers Club.
April 6	The St. Paul Pioneer Press sent a reporter to interview me and take pictures for the up and coming Hall of Fame Induction Dinner.
April 8	Attended C.A.F. annual awards dinner in Golden Valley, MN. I was presented with a Certificate of Merit. Great folks!!!
April 14	I was interviewed on the Al Momberg all night talk show on WCCO radio from 1am to 2am about my being inducted into the Hall of Fame. The audience called in with questions, I had a fun time and I stayed awake through it all!
April 19	Gave a presentation at the Radisson South Hotel n Minneapolis for a Social Service Teachers Seminar with D.J. Voth and three other women veterans.
April 20	My son Arthur, who lost his wife last year, was married to Pam and all my children were home. First time we had all been together since 1979.

April 21   A precious moment in my lifetime. I was inducted
            into the Minnesota Aviation Hall of Fame with all
            my children present. The event was held at the
            Thunderbird Hotel in Minneapolis with the largest
            attendance ever-over 400 people. There were eight
            of us inducted, but only three living. I've lived long
            enough to be an exhibit in the museum! So many
            of my friends and family present to support me.
            I am truly blessed, and as I look at the others who
            are members of the Hall of Fame, I am not only
            humbled, but so grateful for the sacrifices and
            achievements of so many.

April 28   Gave a breakfast presentation to the Minnesota
            Air National Guard Officers Wives Club at the
            Thunderbird Hotel. My friends, Gen. Eugene
            Andriotti and Tim Cosalter (the F-16 pilot who
            gave me the Ride of a lifetime) were present and
            we all had a great time.

April 28   Attended a Women in the Military luncheon/meeting
            at the Veteran's Hospital in Minneapolis and hitched
            a ride home with Joe and Elaine Herda in the
            Faribault Area Veterans Service van.

May 7   Gave a program at the Del Webb Ballroom
            in St. Cloud, MN. for the Metro-Area Veterans
            Association. Wonderful reception, wonderful dinner.

June 15   Mike Vincent from Arizona, a young man interested
16-17   in WW II history, picked up WASP Micky Axton, 99'er
            Bev Turk and myself and drove to Atchison, Kansas
            for the Forest of Friendship Celebration. Faye Gillis
            and eight other Wasp's were in attendance and we
            were honored at the festivities. The air show was
            spectacular and afterwards there was a parade with
            many VIPs. Stopped at Clear Lake, Iowa on return
            trip-Buddy Holly country and site of fatal crash- and
            also saw the Surf Ballroom where Micky's husband,
            a clarinetist, used to entertain. A truly GREAT time.
            Thank you Mike!

June 23   My sister Cecelia, son Patrick and myself attended the
            Wings of Mercy annual banquet at the Air Wings
            Museum in Blaine, MN. Anoka County Airport.
            Northwest pilot Lyle Prouse was the keynote
            speaker, and what a story he had to tell.

June 25	Jean Hardy, who we met at the Wings of Mercy banquet, came to my home to interview me about my flying career. She is a woman pilot, aerobatic instructor from Maine who owns her own airport and is doing a doctoral thesis on women in varying circles of society.
July 2	My son Patrick and myself went to Flemming Field in St. Paul to attend the unveiling of the beautifully restored Red Tail P-51.Mustang of the Tuskegee Airman. This is one of only four of this model still flying. Lee Archer, Tuskegee airman, went for the inaugural ride, and Dr. Harold Brown, who I was with at the "Gathering of Eagles" was also present.
July 13 14-15	Air Expo 2001, one event as part of the Minneapolis Aquatennial Celebration, took place at Flying Cloud Airport. Friday evening was a banquet at the Radisson South Hotel with a cost of $65.00 per person to sit with one of the V.I.P.'s. Thought I would be sitting alone, but actually there was a great turnout. Some of the others involved were Fred Olivi, Ken Dohlberg, Joseph Gomer, Col. Robert Morgan, Micky Axton, the Flying Tigers and many others. I stationed the WASP booth at the air show on Saturday and Sunday. Saw many old friends and met many new ones.
July 19	Gave program to the C.A.P. group at the Burnsville, MN. City Hall. Kathleen Jacobsen was my contact and provided transport.
July 21	Our good friend Don Paquette drove Rose (his wife), my sister Cecelia and myself to the Golden Wings Museum at the Anoka Airport for an 8th Air force dinner party. They flew in a B-17 and a B-24 for the event. What beautiful planes! We were the guests of Larry Bachman who also was keynote speaker.
July 28-29	Managed WASP booth at the Military Expo held at Fort Snelling Base in St. Paul. Micky Axton was with me in the beginning, but the heat was too much. I did stay with her Saturday night, and went to church in Excelsior Sunday morning. Little Andy gave me a ride back to the Base and wonderful Ray Peterson, (who got me the C-130 simulator time) was the narrator for the day and escorted me about.
August 1	The Texas Raiders, of the Confederate Air Force, flew their B-17 to the Owatonna airport adjacent to the

Heritage Halls Museum for a P.R. promotion and advertising the CAF Air show at Flemming Field over the weekend. I was there from 2pm till 5pm hobnobbing and visiting with the public. Great fun giving tours of a beautiful aircraft. Wonderful people that the Raiders are, they called in the evening asking if I might like to fly in the B-17 to Holman Field in St. Paul and back on Thursday for a media promotion or the upcoming air show. Well what do you think I said? You bet!!!

August 2   Arrived at Owatonna Airport at 9:30am for the trip. Someone had to cancel their ride, so there was room for my son, Patrick. All either one of us could say was WOW! Pat flew in the nose as bombardier and, after airborne, they let me fly as first pilot to St. Paul. After 57 years I was once again flying a B-17. After arriving at Holman Field we picked up some media people and did an aerial photo shoot. Along on the run was a WW II pilot who flew the B-I7 at Las Vegas in 1943 while I was a co-pilot. I am so blessed to have so many wonderful friends who let me do these things. May God bless the Texas Raiders.

August 3   Friday evening we enjoyed a banquet at the CAF Hangar #3 at Flemming Field to kick off the weekend air show. Byron and Celia Moon were among the dignitaries. After dinner, there was an interview hosted by Mike Woodley from WMNN radio. The panel was quite an impressive group: Paul Tibbetts, B-29 pilot of the Enola Gay that dropped the bomb on Hiroshima, Bill Bower, B-25 pilot attached to the Doolittle Raiders, Lee Archer, Tuskegee Airman, and Lt. Com. Bob Carlson, on board the USS Oklahoma at Pearl Harbor. Their stories border on the fantastic, unbelievable, spine chilling moments of WW II. I was honored and humbled to be in their company. Had WASP booth next to Women In Military and the Minnesota Aviation Hall of Fame during two days of the air show. What a show! Some of the planes on the field were P-51's, AT-6's, a B-25, the B-17, an A-20, C-130 and a DC-3. So many others. Not only the sight of these beautiful craft, but oh the sound as they take off and land. I was truly on cloud 9.

August 7   Patrick drove Cece and myself to Bemidji, MN to visit
8 & 9   our friend and high school classmate Larry Erie and his wife Gladys. They run a bible camp for children on Lake Dellwater, north of Bemidji, and we stayed in

the lodge. Wild, wonderful storms both nights we were there. Had to go to the basement one night because of tornado warnings. Thunder and lighting like you read about! Larry had arranged for me to give my program for the Lion's Club at the noon luncheon after which he gave us the grand tour of Bemidji. At 4:30pm we went to the American Legion Club to give my program to a joint meeting of the Legion and VFW after their dinner/banquet. Such a warm, interested group of people. Scott Hellzen from WCCO TV was there to record the evening for the news. He sent me a copy of the tape. Such a nice young man.

August 11   99 member Debbie Debbel with her husband and 4 children came to my home for lunch before we all went off to the Heritage Halls Museum and Hall Of Fame Exhibit in Owatonna. Had a wonderful visit, and the children were just a delight.

August 13   My WASP friend Pat Young's daughter Patty and her daughter Kylie stopped by for lunch and an update on what us "old" pilots were up to on their way from Duluth to Missouri to visit Pat. We chatted and had a wonderful lunch.

August 24   Patrick drove me to Micky Axton's house in Eden Prairie where our dear friend, Dick Williams, picked us up and drove us to Duluth for an Air Show. We enjoyed a welcoming 'cocktail party' with the Blue Angels, the Red Barron (Stearmans), and Gene Soucy, a three-time U.S. Grumann "Showcat". Gene also did a solo act in a 300xs and performed an inverted ribbon-cut. Spectacular! The CAF from Mesa, Arizona brought their B-17, Sentimental Journey, and a P-51. The Canadian Air Force had a CF-18 with Rick "Slick" Williams Great Air Show. Jean London, A W.A.S.P. from Brainerd MN, joined us on Saturday and Sunday. The Bong Exhibit people were present promoting the Richard Bong Museum being built in Superior Wisconsin. They have my name along three others on a marker they have on sale hoping to attract funds for this wonderful museum. I have donated some items to be displayed along with a video of an interview I gave. Ray Kowsloski, Executive Director of the Duluth Air Port, invited me to view the Sunday air show from the tower. I could almost reach out and touch the Blue Angels as they blew by! Dick drove us back to Minneapolis later on Sunday where Patrick and Becky picked me up. I was so excited to share my adventures and felt like I was still in the tower. Most memorable weekend. I do love an air show.

Sept. 7	We had our 1937 Class Reunion at the Evergreen Knoll in Faribault and my sister Cecelia came with me. It is always heart-warming and comforting to chat with friends of a lifetime.
Sept. 8	My sister Cecelia had her 1939 Class Reunion and I tagged along. Again seeing many old and dear friends.
Sept. 10	I gave a program for Lori Dolan's home school group at the Baptist Church in Prior Lake, MN. Such a wonderful group of children and adults.
Sept. 11	The horrendous horrors of tragedy in New York shocked our world and opened a door to a puzzling and uncertain new era. An event I am afraid I will never fully understand. Life as we knew it took on a shadowy, different perspective and made me more fully appreciate our recent reunions and every day activities. May God bless us, each and every one.
Sept. 14	Our Faribault Airport had an open house for school children to learn about aviation while kicking off our annual Balloon Rally. The attendance and interest were encouraging and the television coverage was informal and a lot of fun.
Sept. 15	Though the weather did not cooperate to launch the balloons, the crowds showed up nonetheless. 20 beautifully colored balloons were present and the awesome 'night glow' was thrilling. Another highlight of Saturday was the wedding of a man and woman balloonist. What an uplifting occasion. My sister Cecelia and I were invited to the reception and post-wedding festivities and had a fabulous time.
Sept. 22	Our Faribault was host for a Boy Scout Jamboree. The weather was nasty so most of our day was spent inside the main hangar. The Civil Air Patrol was present to help with parking and police the airfield. I gave interviews and answered questions for many of the scouts. After all that had happened recently, it was reassuring seeing this great group of kids.
Sept. 22	In the evening, Pat drove Cece, our friend Ruth Brodd and myself to the Hangar Dance sponsored by the Southern Minnesota Wing of the Confederate Air Force in their hangar at Flemming Field. The Big Band swing sound was toe-tapping super as we saw and talked to so many friends.

Sept. 24   Attended the Senior Adults Learning Together
            (S.A.L.T.) luncheon at the Church of the Risen Savior
            in Burnsville, MN. I gave my program as the featured
            speaker to a most receptive audience. Saw so many
            old friends and made many new ones.

Sept. 27   I was interviewed for 3 hours by Thas Saylor,
            a researcher for the Minnesota Historical Society,
            who was taping interviews on W.W. II veterans
            and their stories. Quite a session.

Oct. 2   Shelly Albers contacted me to present my slides
            to her Women's Club. We had a delicious meal
            and my program was well received with many
            questions about my duties during the war and
            women's rights in general.

Oct. 8   Gave program to the University of Minnesota Elder
            Hostel group at the Radisson Hotel in St. Paul.
            Special audience & great dinner in a beautiful setting.

Oct. 10   Gave my program to the folks at Pleasant View
            Estates retirement center and nursing home.
            Knew many residents and enjoyed the interaction.

Oct. 12   Attended the banquet for the Association of Naval
            Aviators at the Fort Snelling Officers Club. It was
            their 'flight jacket' night when all the boys wear their
            old jackets for the evening. They all look just great!
            Mrs. Kruse and myself were the judges and what
            a difficult job. Cece and Patrick accompanied me.

Oct. 15   Was invited to give my program to the Edina
            Women's' Club at the Church of Christ. Delicious
            luncheon, fascinating women and warm reception.
            I sold some books and was invited back.

Oct. 22   Talked to the students from the Alternative High
            School in Northfield, MN at the Community Center.
            A very inquisitive group asking many questions about
            the slides and life during the war.

Oct. 27   Attended the Past Presidents luncheon of the
            American Legion Auxiliary held at the Evergreen
            Knoll Supper Club in Faribault.

Oct. 30   Called members of the District One Hospital Auxiliary
            to donate time or baked goods for our Bake Sale.

Nov. 5	I was Chairman for our American Legion Auxiliary luncheon meeting.
Nov. 8	Presented my slide show to Ed Hanson's EAA chapter in Richfield, MN.
Nov.12	Gave program to Southview Middle School in Edina, MN.
Nov. 13	Gave a program to a Seniors Club in Cannon Falls, MN.
Nov. 15	Gave program to the Kiwani's Club here in Faribault at the Truckers Inn Restaurant at 6:30 A.M. They had a special treat for me in honor of my 82nd Birthday.
Nov. 17	Presented slide show to the Women in the Military at the Veterans Hospital in Minneapolis. Jeff Olson, Commissioner of Veteran Affairs, was present along with our usual great turnout.
Nov. 19	Gave my program to the University of Minnesota Elderhostel arranged again by my friend and coordinator extraordinaire, Jeanne Schwartz. My sisters Cecelia and Julie and my son Patrick escorted me.
Nov. 29	Gave my program to Elmer Barta's Rotary Club in New Prague, MN. Very well received by a very interesting group.
Dec. 3	My last Minnesota outing was to our American Legion Auxiliary meeting before leaving for California for the winter.

TO DATE: Elizabeth has been invited to 18 different states to present her slide show and still going strong!

55TH W.A.S.P. Reunion

This was a 5-day (Oct. 3rd thru 8th) gathering of our girls in Texas. Right from the 'git-go'I was in for an exciting outing. I was to fly to Shreveport, Louisiana and meet up with my friend Charlene Crager and drive down to Dallas. As I arrived at Char's house in my taxi, her neighbor came over to greet me and let me know that Char was in the hospital with a bronchial problem. He helped me get settled in and I took her car to head over to the hospital. And there I find Char, checked in and plugged into the oxygen! She said there was no way she was missing this reunion and that I was to return in the morning and liberate her. That next morn I picked her up with an oxygen tank and a promise to have her back on Monday.

Charlene Crager

So off we go to Dallas complete with the tank. We traveled on to the Blugg-Huey Library at Texas Women University in Denton. They are collecting W.A.S.P. papers, pictures and other memorabilia. We had panel discussions, videos were shown and a memorial service was held in honor of all classes. A statue of a WASP, designed and created by Dottie Swain Lewis, was dedicated on the campus. There were about 500 in our group of WASPs, KOWs (Kids of WASPs) and friends.and about 300 of us stayed in the dormitories and ate in the cafeteria. Just like being in school again!

On Thursday we were bused to Sweetwater, home of Avenger Field, the one and only all women airfield ever in the world:

our training base. Talk about a Sentimental Journey and wonderful homecoming! This is where most of the 1074 women pilots received their WASP wings after ground school and basic, primary and advanced flying all at this one field. The site of Avenger Field is now Texas State Technical College with a WASP museum, memory lane, a walk of honor and our "wishing well" is still collecting coins for good luck on that next test.

Receptions were held and reminiscences were shared. The highlight of our stay was the unveiling of a Texas Historical Commission Marker memorializing Cornelia Clark Fort, the first woman pilot to die while on active duty. At age 24, Cornelia died when her B-13 aircraft collided in mid-air with another plane. The presentation given by Capt. Kim Monroe, age 26 and a B-1 pilot, was touching, moving and uplifting. A fly-over by a B-1 bomber, with an all women crew, brought about that spine-tingling moment of awe we feel on those rare occasions. Our Sweetwater hostesses and hosts truly gave us the Royal, red-carpet treatment and were exceptional.

On Saturday about 150 of us traveled on to Midland Air Field and were greeted by Bob Rice of the C.A.F. That evening there was a reception held in our honor that again reminded us of where we had been some 60 years ago. We absolutely enjoyed the great C.A.F. air show on Sunday along with many friends from Minnesota and a few from England. Small world. Had lunch on the flight line and again were given the Royal treatment.

The Memorial Wall with all our names

One side note: When we arrived in Dallas on Tuesday, the temperature was 90 degrees. On Saturday in Midland the temperature was 19 degrees with wind chill!! Brrr. Who was prepared for that? Every booth that sold jackets or sweat shirts sold out. But we had a wonderful time anyway.

For each one of us, whether standing, wheelchair bound, cane supported or oxygen using, this Reunion was more than extra special. It renewed lifetime friendships, rekindled the spirit of the 40's and truly was our Sentimental Journey.

Remember my friends, my generation is in the past. The future of our great, free nation is in the hands of our children. Protect and nurture them. Teach them the price of freedom. The horizons are boundless. Encourage them to be the best at whatever they choose and to always follow their dreams.

Elizabeth Strohfus

The WASP Memorial

About the author. Patrick Roberts,
Liz's son, returned to Minnesota from
California for a two week vacation
in1996 and got hooked. Between
family home healthcare needs and other
worthwhile opportunities, he has been
in position to escort Liz on many of
her of her outings and been present
to chronicle her story. Having heard
stories from other veterans and their
contributions to the war effort, he
is currently working on a book about
the 455th Servic Squadron/New Guinea
and nose art specialist, Frank Seigert.

Printed in the United States
by Baker & Taylor Publisher Services